MANUFACTURED ENERGY

Using Your Trauma to Fuel a Brighter, Healthier Future

RON LOTTI

"Meet Ron, listen to his incredible story, and learn from him. You will come out of it a much better person — I know I have."
— DAVID E.

"Ron has taken the hand that he was dealt and used it to fuel his drive for success in all facets of life. Ron's story allows people to see that you can rise above your anger, hurt, and frustration to better not only yourself but those around you."
— KELLY G.

"Ron has a habit of helping you realize your true potential within yourself."
— JAMES T.

"Ron is the definition of true grit and perseverance. "
— JUSTIN F.

Manufactured Energy © Copyright 2021 Ron Lotti

Cover design by Stephanie Lynch

DEDICATION

This book is dedicated to the single parents performing miracles everyday by providing for their children and being role models, even if they don't realize that they are. To the men and women who suffer from anxiety, depression, and PTSD, but still find a way to get out of bed and be there for loved ones. For those who believe life is about helping others by being the best versions of themselves possible. To those who have always believed in me and gave me reason to believe in myself. And, most of all, to those people who I love with all my heart but unfortunately pushed away or hurt while battling my own inner demons.

TABLE OF CONTENTS

PREFACE

As a thirty-nine-year-old who owns multiple businesses, has a beautiful family, great friends, and has to operate with a high level of energy every day, I have often been asked how I do it? How do I always have such a positive outlook on life and seem to always have enough energy to fill a room? How am I able to accomplish so many things and have so much "on my plate" all the time?

It's always been difficult, awkward, and (sometimes) embarrassing for me when I get asked those questions. I struggle with it for many reasons.

One, I don't feel very successful at all. I know I have made a TON of mistakes, hurt a lot of people, and have failed to reach many of my goals. I am constantly worried about having enough money to provide for my family. I always feel that I am living a dream and I can't possibly be where I am in life now and I never feel like I am doing enough to be considered a successful person.

Two, my mind is ALWAYS filled with negative thoughts. I am jealous of just about everyone, wishing I looked better, was stronger, had more money, could be as funny or as smart as someone else, and the list goes on forever. I assume everyone is out to get me and that the world is simply one huge conspiracy theory trying to ruin everyone's lives, starting with mine. I know "for sure" that whatever I am going try to do will definitely fail and that I am going to end up homeless, alone, and broken.

And lastly, I struggle, almost every single morning of my life, to get out of bed. I am surrounded by a shadow, that feels more like a massive storm, of depression and anxiety. I have also been diagnosed with PTSD. There are times when I can actually hear myself, in my own mind, telling me that life isn't worth it and giving me the advice to end it all. I fight urges to drive off a highway into a wall or simply run away without every saying a word to anyone. My depression has been so bad that I have been out of work for months at a time, gone weeks without showering and days without eating, and I was too afraid to fall asleep because I couldn't handle the nightmares I was having.

So, while I am honored to have people compliment me from time to time, I often leave the conversation confused, lost, and wondering if they "know" I am a fraud.

I have spent years with all of this shame filling my mind and holding it all in. I was afraid to admit I had anxiety and depression. I never knew how to explain what PTSD was (still is) doing to me from time to time. I would simply go to a "dark place" and sit there, alone, with my thoughts...hoping the storm would pass.

As I finally started talking to professionals and friends about my thoughts and feelings, I began to realize how much it helped and also how many other people deal with the same things I do.

I began to explain myself as a locomotive engine that simply needs to constantly be in motion, otherwise my thoughts, fears, and anxieties take over and it's nearly impossible to get me going. That's when I decided to explain to people who ask "how I do it" that its "Manufactured Energy." (Hence the name of this book).

Manufactured energy is like shoveling coal into a massive locomotive engine. You have to constantly shovel more and more in to keep it going. It's the ability and necessity, to pick yourself up out of bed and force the energy to come out. It's the constant awareness of your energy levels, your mindset, and your need to keep the engine moving. Manufactured energy is a conscious decision to keep moving forward and embrace the "suck" that you are feeling, knowing you have people in your life that need you...beginning with YOU.

I decided to write this book for a couple reasons.
- I know getting some of this out of my head will eventually help me cope and recover from my past.
- I also know that being productive helps continue to manufacture energy and keep the locomotive moving forward.

Most importantly, though, is my hope that others will read this and know that they are not alone. Maybe, just maybe, everything I went through in my life will help one person get through their own struggles and it will help me feel that I lived through it all for a reason.

Over the next few pages, I will take you into my mind, through something that has helped me my entire life- quotes. I will let you know what each quote means to me and give you some insight into my past, my present, and hopefully, my future.

So, in the words of the great Dr. Dre, "journey with me into the mind of a maniac."

CHAPTER 1

EMBRACE THE SUCK

Face Your Demons Head On

"You cannot defeat darkness by running from it, nor can you conquer your inner demons by hiding them from the world. In order to defeat the darkness, you must bring it into the light."
— SETH ADAM SMITH

Such a powerful quote and very meaningful to me. I've been fighting the demons since I was a kid. Haunted by tragic and horrific events I witnessed. I was constantly living in fear when I was a kid. Fear of someone hurting me was part of it, but fear of someone hurting my mother or, even worse, watching my mother hurt herself. I witnessed it repeatedly. From the beatings (stepfathers and others hitting me and my mother), to being tied up and left in a burning house, and everything in between. But, far worse than any of it, and what still haunts me today, was watching my mother physically, mentally, and emotionally destroy herself over time using drugs and alcohol.

I am haunted by the memories of watching a beautiful, smart, and caring human being lose the battle of addiction and turn into a fearful, angry, depressed, suicidal, and many times ugly and dark, person.

While I have come a long way in getting through the pain and moving forward in life, the demons are always still there… watching and waiting. Last night, unfortunately, they attacked in my dreams.

I had a nightmare in which I bumped into my mother at a bar while I was on my way home from work. At first, I didn't think she was really there, but then she gave me the look I remember so vividly (and it's been just under fifteen years since I've seen her), that said "it's me, and I'm sorry." I went over to talk with her and, before I could say a word, she said "I've been hoping to find the right time to say I'm sorry and that I have changed, I think it's time."

I was in shock and just sat there. We both started to cry, while the bar was suddenly filling up with a lot of people. I didn't recognize anyone in the bar but did notice it was VERY dark.

Not long after being there, my mother said she had to go to the bathroom but would be right back. As she walked away, an undercover police officer came over to me and said, "I am right around the corner if you need anything."

As my mother came back to our table, I noticed something was off. I could see in her eyes that she was high. She had gone to the bathroom and shot up. She tried to pretend she was fine. When I called her out on it, she denied doing anything. But I knew the look in her eyes.

We argued for a few moments until she finally said, "this is who I am, and you need to accept it." That's when I hugged her, cried on her shoulder, but then walked away from the table to the front of the building, calling the undercover police officer over. I told him she was high and that I needed to go. He said he would take care of it.

I glanced over at my mother, one last time, crying and shaking. She gave me one more look, telling me she knew and understood. Then I walked out of the bar, stepped on a bus, and told the driver to take me anywhere he wanted, I just needed to go away.

I woke up soaking wet, tears in my eyes and feeling very weak. The very thought of the sight of those eyes still gives me chills to this day. It's hard to believe that, after years and years of fighting this battle, mentally, that it's all still there, lurking.

Thankfully, I began to forgive my past and tell my story a few years ago. Opening and allowing the demons to show their faces, come into the light, has helped my healing process, and allowed me to grow.

I believe this nightmare was just another way of me bringing the demons out of the darkness and continuing down my path of forgiveness.

My hope is that, not only will I continue to grow and release my mind from the demons that haunt me from my childhood, but that telling my story and sharing my thoughts will help someone else feel comfortable doing the same and begin the journey of forgiveness and healing.

~ ~ ~ ~ ~ ~ ~ ~

Everyone faces challenges at some point in life, some harder than others. Some of the challenges can be traumatic and painful. Those are the challenges that tend to stick with you and can sometimes try to take control of your mind, forcing negative and depressing thoughts upon you. Those are the challenges I call my "demons."

As painful as they are, I do believe those demons are also what push me to find strength, courage, and hope in my life. By allowing yourself to feel the pain and then talk about the demons, letting them out into the light instead of just hiding deep down in the darkness within you, will help to overcome them and keep them at bay.

"Feeding" the demons with more negative, more darkness, and isolation will only give them more power over you. Every day is a new test and new chance to overcome them.

Face the demons head on, talk about the pain and suffering the memories caused you, and allow yourself to forgive the past so you can find joy in the present and future.

**"Sometimes it's hard to wake up in the mornin'.
Mind full of demons, I don't wanna hear 'em
anymore." — TUPAC**

While I find myself focusing on the positive as much as possible and working towards my goals, I'd be lying if I said the demons of my childhood and the depression, anxiety, and PTSD of my life suddenly disappeared.

We all hear the stories of men and women who fought though horrible events in their lives, developed depression, anxiety, and depression but ultimately achieved amazing things. Those same people tend to stand on stage and share their stories or we hear them on podcasts talking about how they have overcome so many things to be where they are in life now. They also spend time sharing HOW they got to where they are and what drives them even more in their present lives.

What we tend NOT to hear is how they STILL deal with the demons. They still struggle with depression, anxiety, PTSD, and other difficult symptoms. These issues do not simply disappear one day and all is right with the world.

I still have many days that I wake up, have an enormous feeling of depression and it's like I am stuck in my bed. I'm afraid to get up. I feel failure, shame, resentment, anger, sadness, and almost every other negative emotion possible – all at the same time. It can be paralyzing at times. I find that I simply want to stay there and cry all day. I want to isolate myself from the world, keep it as dark as possible in my room, and completely give up or shut down.

Most people never see that side of me. They see me post on social media or hear me talk about how much work I put into my day or of the goals I "crushed" that day and they believe all must be great for me. What they do no not realize is how much effort I had to put in to just getting out of bed. I had to do everything possible to build up enough energy and courage to face the day.

I live with thoughts of fear and doubt, shame and grief, sadness and remorse, insecurity and anger every single moment of my life. I've made mistakes because I acted out in anger or tried to sabotage my life. I have lost many great friends and ruined relationships with loved ones. This all simply causes more shame and regret.

Thankfully, this is a battle I have gotten used to fighting. That alone, being willing to fight the battle, took me many years to be willing to do. There was a time that I wouldn't get out of bed. I wouldn't face the world or try to move past my internal and invisible struggles.

I am determined to continue to grow as a person and face the demons every single day. I allow myself to recognize that they are there, and that they always will be. I just decided to give them as little space in my mind as possible. I give them about five minutes to be present, tell them it's time to move on, and then get my ass out of bed and try to find the smallest goal to achieve as possible so I can begin to build positive momentum for the day. Getting dressed, eating breakfast, reading a book, going for a walk, or even going straight to my gym all help me get started.

While the demons of my past may always be with me, I now realize that I can control how much strength I allow them to have over me. This battle is one I will face for the rest of my life but it's my goal to win more battles than I lose and I am forever thankful for the lessons I have learned throughout the many wars within I have faced.

~ ~ ~ ~ ~ ~ ~ ~ ~

I'd normally discuss some lessons learned and ways to overcome the challenges you face here, but I want to encourage all of you to help support those you know, and may not know, who are dealing with depression, anxiety, PTSD, and other invisible battles.

It's truly impossible for you to ever know what the person in front of you is struggling with or has faced at one point in their lives. All you can do is be open-minded to the fact that they are struggling. Show empathy as often as you can and offer to help, while realizing they may not yet be ready for your help.

Please support great causes like the following (and many more that may not be listed):

- **Mission 22**
  https://www.mission22.com

- **Mental Health Association**
  https://www.mharochester.org

- **Anxiety and Depression Association of America**
  https://adaa.org

- **The Jed Foundation**
  https://www.jedfoundation.org

- **PTSD Alliance Partners**
  http://www.ptsdalliance.org/partners

I've been given so many opportunities in my life to grow as a person and develop some amazing skills – specifically coping skills, stress management, and life skills. Many times, though, I let life punch me in the mouth and then mope around complaining or doing nothing about it. I feel fortunate to be able to make that decision -learn from it or mope around.

For the longest time, I looked at my childhood as something that happened to me and in a VERY negative light. I spent years in counseling trying to get out all my anger and sadness. I'd spend hours talking about how "this person did this to me, and then this fell apart," or how "witnessing these things caused me to feel this way, which is why I am unable to do "X" now."

But, just this week... during all of the worldwide pandemic issues, economic crises, and even my 12-year-old dog developing a cancerous tumor causing us to have to put her down, I decided to look back on my life and realize how it was a gift preparing me for every single stressful or depressing moment I would face for the rest of my life.

I've been able to keep my head up and be there for my wife, daughter, and friends over the last couple weeks. I intend on being the rock that others need while also allowing myself to feel the emotions I am feeling, in a healthy way, for the rest of my life.

I've taken every punch that I have been hit with, and decided to react in a positive, inspiring, and momentum building way. I have the skills to overcome all of this BECAUSE of what I witnessed as a kid. I survived shit I probably shouldn't have survived because I was meant to be strong NOW. I am thankful for all that I went through and will use it all, along with every other punch I ever take, to become a better person, father, husband, and friend.

~ ~ ~ ~ ~ ~ ~ ~

We all get to choose how we react to every situation we encounter in our lives. One of the shitty parts about this world is that it simply waits for no one. You can sit around and dwell on the shitty situation you are in or you can decide to pick your ass up and do something positive with it.

Your reaction is what will determine the outcome, not only in the short term but for the rest of your life. Build up a strong discipline of how you will react. Take a moment to uncover every single emotion you are feeling, decision that needs to be made, and options available. Then, after a moment, take a breath and move forward on the path that gets you closer to a better situation. Think of the people around you who depend on you, think of why you do what you do, and focus on all the potential positive outcomes. Then...go make it happen. Be the person you want to be, regardless of what you have been dealt.

"You can either be the victim of your life or the master of it. The choice is yours." – UNKNOWN

I spent ages two to age fifteen moving, watching drugs and alcohol destroy my family, and wondering (most days) if I would survive another day. I had multiple stepfathers use me as a punching bag, my mother and her friends would dress me up and make fun of the way I looked, I witnessed my mother being beaten and raped by multiple people, and many other horrific events.

Witnessing things that I wouldn't wish upon my worst enemy built up a lot of fear, anger, and resentment. I had a massive chip on my shoulder for many years and found myself asking, "Why did all of that happen to me? What did I do to deserve all of that?"

I spent many years feeling guilty, wishing for a "better life," and feeling jealous of everyone I saw having a "better life" than me. Most of these emotions came out as anger when I was in high school. I had a very hard time listening to teachers telling me what to do. This concept was foreign to me, as I barely had anyone at home who cared what I was doing, or not doing, every day. Why would I listen to whatever this person, who barely knew me, was telling me to do? It didn't matter if it was my teacher, a coach on any team I played for, someone in administration at the school, or even police officers in town. I was angry at the world, felt like the world "owed" me an explanation, and simply didn't want to do anything to better myself.

Finally, after moving in with a friend and his family my sophomore year of high school, I started to turn it around. I started listening to the advice others had given me that I can become something more and be successful in life IF I work hard and really want to. I started to write out goals for myself and was absolutely determined to build my life up to something that I would be proud of.

I stopped blaming the world for my problems, stopped allowing myself to sit in self-pity, and stopped playing the victim card. I would never again sit back and just watch the world "happen to me." I would spend my days working towards my goals and become someone that would inspire other people. I made it my personal goal to use everything I went through as a kid as my fuel that keeps me driving towards my goals, to help, to empower, and to inspire people to become the best versions of themselves and leave a legacy that people I care about will be happy to talk about long after I am gone.

While I have had many times throughout the years that I've fallen backwards or been stuck in an emotional rut for longer periods of time than I would like, I have never fallen back further than where I began this journey. Yes, there are many things I wish I had done differently, but I can say for certain that I have inspired many people and will continue to live my best life moving forward, making a massive positive impact on this world.

~ ~ ~ ~ ~ ~ ~ ~ ~

Unfortunately, too many people sit back, playing the victim of their own lives, and wait for great things to happen to them. Or worse, spend every day BLAMING the world for their problems instead of doing anything about it.

While I can understand getting angry at your situation, or wishing things were better, I cannot understand the mentality of simply doing nothing to better yourself or playing the victim card for your entire life. This does you, and no one else, any good and will get you absolutely nowhere in life. Stop making excuses and take action.

People are far too distracted in the world today and, instead of making progress in life, would rather spend hours on social media complaining (along with everyone else) about their lives. Until you are willing to cut negativity out of your life and surround yourself with positive action, nothing will change.

From now on, give yourself about five minutes to complain about your overall situation and then decide that shit is over, time to move on. Remove all distractions, determine you are no longer a victim, and make the decision to build the life you want to build. Let everyone who does not help you along in your journey fall by the wayside. You deserve better. Get up and get going now because no one else will do it for you, nor should they. It's your life and it's your story. Now, get started writing it.

"If you are depressed you are living in the past. If you are anxious you are living in the future. If you are at peace you are living in the present."
— LAO TZU

Depression, because of my past, is something I have lived with my entire life, but anxiety is something that has, lately, been kicking my ass. One of the wonderful thoughts my anxiety brings me is that I am running out of time in my life. I feel the burning desire to make the most of every single day, but then look back and think "man...that wasn't enough!" and it causes me to lose sleep. In fact, I woke up at 1:30am today, got out of bed at 2:30am and began stressing about every single aspect of my life. This, unfortunately, is a common occurrence.

I worry about having enough money to provide for my family. I worry that I am not making a big enough positive impact on the world and will not be remembered. I worry that I will fail, at everything, and lose everything I have in life. These thoughts wake me up in the middle of the night, they hold me tight to the bed and make it difficult to get up, and they creep in all throughout my day.

No matter the accomplishments I have made in my life, no matter how many times I am told positive things about myself, and no matter how many obstacles I find a way to overcome… the darkness within constantly pulls me down and gives me things to worry about

This morning, for the first time, I forced myself to focus on one small thing at a time, the PRESENT. I literally started by saying, "For the next few minutes, focus on breathing correctly." That's all, just breathing. When thoughts started to creep in, I (internally) yelled at myself to stay focused.

My heart rate slowed down, and I began to relax. Then I let myself make a short list, just three things, that I would focus on throughout the day and not allow myself to do anything else until I accomplished those three things.

My list:
1.   Stick with my fitness challenge and not miss a day
2.   Write a short portion of this book

3.   Help my wife and daughter clean the house

Everything started to feel a little better. I told myself "When I accomplish those three things, I will have fulfilled my goal of making a positive impact, spending time with people I love, and feeling accomplished."

~ ~ ~ ~ ~ ~ ~ ~ ~

Living in the present moment is something we all say and hear from experts. It's so very easy to say, but unbelievably difficult to accomplish. That said, the less we focus on our present, the more anxiety and depression we could be causing for ourselves.

When we miss out on all the greatness that surrounds us every day, we will look back and feel guilty, causing depressed feelings in the future. If we only think or worry about the future, it will never come. We will be so focused on later, that we will miss now, and anxiety will reign supreme in our thoughts.

Take moments, throughout the day, to make yourself "smell the roses" and embrace the present moment. Set up calendar meetings for yourself to force it to happen. Hug your spouse and kids, pets your dogs, write down 1-2 things about your current life that you are grateful for.

None of us know how many days or moments we have left. Embrace the moments you are currently living and feel the joy that each moment brings you. One way to never look back and wonder "if" is to make every moment you are living now count.

Enjoy it and it will bring more joy in the future, without having to worry about what might come next.

"In each of us, two natures are at war — the good and the evil." – ROBERT LOUIS STEVENSON

There is certainly a constant battle going on in my mind, and it's been there since I was a kid. I find myself having to fight off the desire to flip out, throw things, and run away. I've spent a good portion of my life wondering how I am still alive, telling myself I don't deserve anything, and that I should just give up. But then I have a ton of moments when I am fully motivated, feel like I worked my butt off to be where I am in life, and want nothing more than to make a positive impact on everyone around me.

What makes all of this even more difficult is that I dwell on the fact that I face these struggles and feel ashamed of it. "Am I crazy?", "What the hell is wrong with me?", "How could I possibly have these thoughts?", "Do I not appreciate my life?"

For most of my life, I kept ALL these thoughts to myself. I told no one that I spent a good portion of the night scared, in bed, because I just had a horrible dream or that all I wanted to do was destroy everything in my life. I tried to figure it all out on my own. I felt that only weak people have trouble dealing with this stuff, I must not be strong enough. It's basically felt like a constant battle to either become something great or fall down into something VERY dark.

~ ~ ~ ~ ~ ~ ~ ~

Recently, I began using the battle within to help me grow as a person. It motivates me to push myself. I've learned to listen to what I am feeling and make decisions based off which side is "winning." When the dark side is taking over, it's time to elevate my energy level, communicate the issue to my close friends and family, and list out a couple things to accomplish that will work in my favor. When the "good" side is taking over, that's when mountains need to be moved, goals need to be crushed, and charitable work needs to be done. I embrace the energy, on either side, and push it to work FOR me, not AGAINGST me.

This new way of reacting did not happen overnight. It has taken years of writing in a gratitude book, attempting new career endeavors, and (most importantly) talking to someone about it. Discussing the inner thoughts and the inner battle, explaining that there just seems to always be a shadow waiting behind me, and allowing myself to FEEL what those energies make me feel have helped me tremendously.

There has been a ton of trial and error, and there will continue to be moving forward, but allowing myself to be who I am (knowing that there is a constant battle within) has helped me become who I want to be.

**"History doesn't repeat itself,
but it often rhymes." – MARK TWAIN**

I find myself falling in and out of "ruts" from time to time. Sometimes the rut is far deeper than other, but the feelings are quite the same, I feel stuck, unmotivated, and sometimes lost. In the past, this rut has led to prolonged periods of depression.

Times when I struggled to get out of bed, never wanted to eat, and did everything I could to ruin great relationships I had in my life. I would quit a job or intentionally destroy something I had been working on, only hoping to get fired. I would argue with loved ones over things that didn't matter, hoping to escalate it to a point that they would no longer want to be in my life.

I basically felt like my world was too good for me, like I was living a dream. I never felt good enough for the people that were in my life, or for the career I had, or the successes I found along the way. I found myself waiting for the floor to fall out from underneath me and someone to say, "see, I told you it was all too good to be true." No matter what I accomplished, or how many people told me how important I was to them, I simply never internalized it and certainly never believed it to be true.

This feeling, unfortunately, hasn't gone away. It has gotten "quieter", but it hasn't completely left the building. It feels like a shadow constantly following me around and waiting for something to go wrong so that it can swoop and get the ball rolling in the wrong direction.

~ ~ ~ ~ ~ ~ ~ ~ ~

Over the last few years, I started seeking out guidance and support to help me through these times. Thankfully, I have received some great guidance. One of the best pieces of advice I have gotten, though very difficult to go through, was to look back on my past and allow myself to feel what I was going through once again. Only, this time, bring it back to what is different in my life now.

For example, as a child I experienced a lot of difficult and challenging moments. Many of those times, I simply couldn't control any part of it and didn't realize what was going on. Now, as an adult, the major difference is my ability to control some of the situations and even avoid them all together. Also, realistically, I will never have to face any of those situations again because of the growth I have experienced in my life and the positive choices I have made.

I relate it to being on a plane. As a child, I wouldn't get to choose my flight, my seat, or my destination...an adult in charge of me would. Now, as the adult, I can decide which flight I take, where I sit, where my destinations is, etc. I allow myself to recognize that I have choices, and that is a very liberating feeling.

Looking back, I started to see a bit of a pattern developing prior to falling into the rut. My thoughts would start to become erratic; I would get angered or agitated very easily, and I would crave some sort of big change (move, change jobs, start a completely new workout routine, etc.). I decided to call this "the storm."

When I feel "the storm" coming I allow myself to take a few steps back and start thinking about how the present is different from the past. I let my loved ones know that the storm is coming, and I can feel the clouds getting darker. I trust that they will help me through the storm and even that they will understand that the next few days, or longer, could be a little rough. They understand what could be coming and then challenge my thoughts or actions when I start to react in a negative way. This process tends to repeat itself, but the rut seems to be much shallower each time.

While my history certainly seems to come back time and time again, thankfully I have begun to recognize patterns and develop new ways to approach the similar situations and feelings. By allowing myself to identify similar feelings, reactions, and emotions I have begun to change my outlook on life and truly believe I have grown as a person because of it.

Don't let your past control your future. One way to do this is to never forget your past and allow yourself to "go back" in time and focus on the patterns of what took place. The only way to avoid the past repeating itself it to recognize it happened and learn from it, not by burying it away and pretending it never happened.

"The worst part about being strong is that no one ever asks if you're okay." – UNKNOWN

I've spent the last few weeks focusing on how to be sure I am always appearing strong for everyone in my life. If fact, I feel like I have spent most of my life acting this way. Especially in the face of chaos, I have always felt that it's on me to be sure people get through it. That's nobody's fault but my own. I honestly can say that I enjoy being the person people turn to when they need help.

That said, today was my day to break down. During my second workout, indoors and lifting weights, I literally broke down in tears. I felt the weight of the entire situation, (lock down due to the coronavirus, financial worry due to closing the gym, seeing my daughter trying to go to school online while not spending time with her friends or playing the sport she loves) bearing down on me and just fell to my knees.

This is not the first time it happened to me. It happens quite a bit. I hold it all in and "fake it till I make it" then find myself alone somewhere and break down.

~ ~ ~ ~ ~ ~ ~ ~ ~

For a moment, in my head, I told myself to stop crying and just move on. Then I stopped myself from doing that, and said... this time out loud, "It's ok to feel this way. Everything going on in the world and specifically in my life right now, absolutely justify feeling the way I do. Take a moment and let it out, cry damnit, just be in the moment and feel it."

So, I did. I took a few minutes and just let it all out. I allowed myself to feel sad, to feel worried, and even to feel angry. I cried out loud and into a towel. Then, I took a few deep breaths and thought about all the good in my life. My wife, my daughter, my friends and family, the progress I have made since I was a kid, the goals I have achieved, even my dogs.

Then, out of nowhere, a voice said "These are the moments you were training for throughout your entire life. This is why you faced, and conquered, every challenge you faced as a kid. You were built for this. You ARE THE LION. Only now, you are not alone."

A surge of energy rushed through my body and I jumped back into my workout, excited for an opportunity to continue my journey.

When emotions hit you, and hit you hard, take a moment to recognize it. Think about how you feel, acknowledge that its ok, and allow yourself to "be" in the moment. Forcing it down and out of your thoughts will only prolong the problem. Allow yourself to talk about it and learn from it. Go be the LION in your own life but recognize that even the LION can turn to others in time of need.

"The weak can never forgive. Forgiveness is the attribute of the strong." – MAHATMA GANDHI

It is amazing how much "weight" I've been carrying around in my life due to the anger and resentment I have felt towards my mother and many other people from my childhood. For a long time, I viewed it all as a chip on my shoulder pushing me to move forward in life.

What took me a very long time was to realize that it was actually nothing more than an anchor always with me, keeping me from ever truly being where I want to be in life, happy and content in who I am as a person and able to enjoy all aspects of my surroundings.

It was always much easier for me to simply bury the anger and resentment somewhere deep within, pretending that it had no impact on my thought process or actions. It took many years for me to see how much of a role it played in every aspect of my life. It would creep in whenever things were going well, causing doubt and pain. It would show up when things were not going so well with little remarks like, "I told you."

It stuck around, playing an intricate role in almost all of my decisions and action until I finally decided to face it. For me to move past the anger, hate, and resentment and to truly live my best life, I had to spend hours upon hours reliving many of the details of my past that I had never wanted to think about ever again.

I forced myself to try and put myself in the shoes of those who hurt me. Most of the time spent was thinking about my mother. For many years I walked around extremely angry that she could "ever treat me the way she did" and "choose drugs and alcohol over me." It wasn't until I started to truly try and see it from her point of view that things finally started to change in my life.

I felt pain in my heart while going through this exercise. I couldn't handle the amount of shame she must have felt, every single day. It hurt to think that she was constantly feeling "broken" and "lost." She never felt good enough for anyone and never truly loved herself.

I've cried for hours just thinking of how hard it must have been for her to be in and out of jail or rehab, to watch her children suffering but feel inadequate as a parent, or to feel like no one in the world ever cared if she was alive or not. I found myself wishing she could have just seen herself through my eyes, knowing that she would've see how amazing of a person that she was and maybe not caring so much of what others thought of her.

As painful as it was, and still is, thinking through all of this, it has truly helped me to forgive my mother for the pain I felt as a child. And, since going through this exercise and working on it often, I have finally begun to feel that "anchor" begin to let go. I find myself seeing the world in a different light. Loving myself doesn't seem like such a foreign concept to me anymore and I swear I feel happiness and love much more than I ever have before.

~ ~ ~ ~ ~ ~ ~ ~

It feels so much easier going about your day with the "me against the world" mentality when you are always trying to prove yourself. Somewhere, behind that thinking, is some sort of anger or resentment for something you've gone through in your past.

Having the ability to forgive and move on not only allows you to enjoy your life much more now, it helps prepare you for future challenges you will face.

Not allowing anger, hate, and resentment to anchor your growth and development gives you the strength to face challenges in life head on. It's like going for a long walk uphill. You can choose to wear a 100lb vest of negativity or allow yourself to forgive the people in your past that have hurt you and go on without the vest weighing you down.

Take some time to put yourself in the mindset of those who have wronged you in the past. Try to forgive them for what they had done. Do so, not necessarily for them, but to free yourself from that burden. And then, go on kicking ass in life, without ever having to look back or feel that pain ever again.

ACTION STEPS

1. **Stop trying to bury the past.** Pushing the memories away and never facing them head on will only cause more issues later in life. Find a way to let out the negative experiences you went through. Journal, voice recordings, or even long talks with loved ones can be a great way to start.

2. **Get help.** Asking for help is a strength, not a weakness. Seek professional help to work on your mental health. It took me years to realize that I needed to truly open up if I ever wanted to make progress. There are a ton of resources to help you find a professional to talk to. And, like a good friend once told me, therapists are like avocados, not all are going to work for you. Keep looking until you find the right therapist or counselor. I promise there is one out there that will be able to help you.

3. **Allow yourself to forgive those that have wronged you.** The anger, hate, and resentment only hurt you more and certainly do nothing to help you move forward in life. Do not let those who have hurt you in the past continue to take up mental capacity in your life now.

CHAPTER 2

THE WAR IS WITHIN

Mind Your Thoughts

"Whether it's good thoughts or bad thoughts... wherever your mind goes... reality always follows." – ANDY FRISELLA

This quote speaks volumes to me because it's ABSOLUTELY true. When I spend time thinking of the negative crap in my life, past or present, I tend to bring upon negativity and fall down the crap trap. When the head trash of fear, anxious, doubt, or grief take over my thoughts, my life tends to spiral downward and sometimes out of control. It's when I start to shut people out of my life, isolate myself, and ruin all the progress I have built up. I find myself digging deeper and deeper into a hole that, at that moment, seems impossible to climb out of.

When I focus on all the positives in my life and embrace the process to become who I want to be for myself, family, and friends, the positive energy flows and momentum towards everything I want to achieve seems like it's powered by a jet engine. Things just seem easier to do, obstacles seem easier to overcome, and life just feels more joyful.

The struggle, though, is that it can take a bit to realize I am in control of those thoughts. I have the power to think differently, to approach things with a positive mindset, and to alter the current path I am on. It's just a matter of recognizing it much faster, reacting to the cues telling me my mindset is hurting and not helping me, and making a change.

~ ~ ~ ~ ~ ~ ~ ~ ~

Life comes at you fast and it's easy to get caught up in all the bullshit that's thrown at you. I believe the universe is always on your side, helping you to get to where you want to be. But it also will throw a ton of challenges at you in order test you and find out how bad you really want it.

I've begun to approach the negative shit as simply a test. When I wake up and feel like shit, it's the universe whispering in my ear "Hey man, no big deal, go back to sleep...you don't really want that goal, do you?" Or when I find myself getting punched in the face, over and over, with bad news, it's basically just the universe saying "Dude, you sure you want to get back up again?"

Focusing on the positives, saying out loud what your goals are, that you can achieve them plus much more, and telling the universe that you've got this, will do amazing things. Take time, every day, to step back and monitor your thoughts. Are they helping or hurting you? Do they align with what you want in life or are they helping dig the hole of misery? If it isn't helping you to move forward, recognize it, say out loud that it's not who you are or what you want in life, and move the fuck on – further down the path of awesomeness that you are headed towards.

> **"You have power over your mind — not outside events. Realize this, and you will find strength."**
> — MARCUS AURELIUS

For the longest time I felt the need to control as much as I possibly could to feel safe and that everything would be ok. I would limit my experiences and endeavors to things that were familiar to me and therefore not have to worry about the "what-ifs." I never wanted to put myself in uncomfortable situations because I feared I would fail or something bad would happen.

The need for control stunted my growth and never allowed me to find my true potential. Worse than that, I never truly found happiness or fulfillment because I was too afraid to try new things that I could end up really enjoying.

While I would try new things from time to time, I never truly allowed myself to experience them. I wouldn't allow myself to be in the moment or truly open up. I kept my feelings to myself and rarely shared my thoughts, my true thoughts, with others. I felt that I could only keep people close if I portrayed a certain image of who I was, what I thought was a strong minded individual, and never let them see the real me.

What's interesting about my approach was the fact that the only thing I ever controlled was my mindset towards life and every moment that I am living.

Much like the weather, I can't control very much of what's happening around me. I can't control how others react, or their opinions towards certain things. For the longest time I found myself fighting others on their opinions and, rather than focusing on my own mindset or thoughts, tried to change their thoughts.

~ ~ ~ ~ ~ ~ ~ ~

I remember thinking that if I acted a certain way, maybe I could get my mother to stop turning to drugs and alcohol and she would finally be a great mom every day, instead of only sometimes.

I wanted to get straight A's in school so she would see that I was very smart and maybe that would make her love me more and pay more attention to me. I would study all night to pass an exam, but only to get a good grade (never to truly learn the materials or be able to apply it to life.) I'd run home with my papers marked with an "A" hoping to change how my mother would act, only to see her passed out on the floor, drunk and unable to recognize who I was. Therefore, the grades began to not matter to me, and I found that I never even cared, or enjoyed, getting straight "A's" in school.

I would practice my batting wing all day long so that, come game time, I would excel and show my mother that I am a great athlete. I would lead my team in batting average, stolen bases, and make the all star team every year, only to have my mother either show up to games drunk, yelling and screaming until someone asked her to leave, or to have her not show up at all. All the wins, all-star game appearances, and accolades simply meant nothing to me, and I never felt good enough.

All of this carried over into my adult life. I still find myself wanting to "do more" and finding that need to be the best at everything to get any attention. I worry that I am not good enough all the time. I've been fortunate to achieve many great things as an adult, but rarely find myself enjoying the journey or realizing my accomplishments.

I have begun to focus only on my mindset and force myself to take a step back throughout the day to recognize my life and how grateful I am. I take time. every morning, to sit and think about how far I have come. I write out what I am grateful for and excited about every morning. I try to recognize when negative thoughts enter my mind and force myself to change the thinking. I allow myself to recognize the thought, accept that it's there, then change my thinking and focus on the positive.

One piece of great advice I have gotten through the years is to not judge myself for my negative thoughts but to allow myself to notice it's there and ask if what I am thinking is true or not. For example, when I feel like I am not good enough and that people will not like me, I allow myself to recognize I am thinking it.

"Ok, I'm feeling worried about how others feel about me and that I am simply not good enough. Has anyone in my life told me that I am not good enough? Has anyone I currently have in my life told me that I have to prove something to them for them to stay in my life? Could I potentially be feeling this way because of what I witnessed as a child? What would I say to myself if I could go back and talk to my eight-year-old self?"

This process has helped me tremendously and I find that I am enjoying much more of my life today. I recently told my friends that I am able to see much more of my surroundings now. Simple things like the colors of flowers, or the feel of a breeze, are just much more amazing to me. I can feel the positive energy all around me much more than before.

While I still have feelings of inadequacy from time to time, I can push through much better than before and thankfully find myself much happier and fulfilled. By focusing on my own mindset, and controlling my thoughts and outlook, I have begun to find the strength I need to accept my past, enjoy my present, and look forward to my future.

> **"And I hate how you made me question myself**
> **when the problem was you all along." –** A.S.

Confidence in myself and my abilities is something I have struggled with my entire life. No matter how much education I have, or how many achievements I've accomplished, I find myself questioning my abilities far more than I tend to believe in myself.

While I am fortunate to have many people over the last few years express how good I am at certain things or that they wish they had the abilities I have, I always leave those conversations feeling like I must be fooling them, or that there is no way they are telling me the truth – they must just want to be nice to me today.

This struggle is a great friend of Mr. Anxiety and Mr. Depression. Constantly questioning my abilities has me feeling like a fraud most days and wondering what value I bring the world I live in. It also has me assuming "everyone will find me out soon enough" and everything I've worked for in my life will simply collapse around me. Once that happens, the rest of my day or night is spent fighting off the idea that no one likes me, my wife and family will leave me, and I will lose my career. This all leads to immediate depression and miserable thoughts about my future.

Unfortunately, this has been going on since I was a kid. I became very used to the idea that the world will collapse around me and we would have to try and pick up the pieces and start all over. I guess that's just what happens when your mom has drug and alcohol addiction issues, spending multiple months in jail or a rehab facility, causing my sisters and I to have to move, again.

It was difficult to make friends because I never lived somewhere long enough to really connect with anyone. I always felt like a fraud because people were nice to me but didn't really know the truth about my life. I would take on the idea that my home life and the way my mother and multiple new drug-using boyfriends or stepfathers had to be who I was too, right? I simply could not separate the "two worlds" I lived in everyday, my true being of who I was as a person and what I witnessed every day from people who were supposed to care about me and protect me.

How could I possibly believe I had anything to offer the world when I watched my mother choose drugs, alcohol, and any random new guy over me?

Thankfully, I found stability later in my life from great people who were willing to allow me to live with them to finish out my high school years. I got to see what a family is really like. Family dinners that did not involve yelling and screaming or brutal beatings seemed like a fairy tale to me, but this was reality for this family (and most other families in the world). I was given shelter, food, someone to look for when I needed advice, and an opportunity to be a teenager.

That "gift" is what got me to believe that my past, and all the horror I had witnessed, was NOT my reality and it was NOT WHO I WAS. It gave me hope that I could be something much more. It also provided me with time to learn more about who I really was.

The biggest lesson I learned then, which has taken me years to truly comprehend and something I STILL WORK ON EVERY DAY is that the REAL battle I faced daily is with myself and my thoughts towards myself. The only person who can stop me from reaching my goals, so long as I truly work towards them, is ME and ME alone, and it begins with self-confidence.

~ ~ ~ ~ ~ ~ ~ ~

The most terrifying thing in the world is the fact that your mind can completely dictate who you become as a person. The battle is within more than it is external. Spend time focusing on your thoughts and work on staying in the present moment, not allowing yourself to dwell on past turmoils.

Self-confidence starts with an understanding that you are only battling yourself. Do not allow the actions of others to impact your mindset. Most importantly, do not spend your time comparing yourself to other people. If you focus your life on giving it your best, every day, along with driving towards constant improvement through education, hard work, and effort, you need not care what others are doing to find your own happiness.

While the voices inside your head may never truly go away, you can work towards making them a much quieter bunch. You give them power by focusing on what they are saying and believing in the negativity. Never allow negative thoughts the ability to rent space in your mind, there is only so much space available and giving it away should be done at a premium, only things that move you towards your goals.

"Doubt kills more dreams than failure ever will."
— SUZY KASSEM

It's amazing how much our own self-talk and self-doubt stops us from achieving great things in life, or even stops us from ATTEMPTING great things.

Fear of failure has had a tendency of stopping me from trying to do things I may enjoy or love to do, many times throughout my life. For some reason I always found myself worrying that I would fail or look bad in front of others, so I would simply decide NOT to try something. There have been many chances for me to compete in athletic events or a new business venture opportunity that I simply declined. My poor self-esteem has found a way, historically, to take over when I have ideas of trying something new. I'd tell myself all the reasons why I would fail or all the reasons I shouldn't even try. I would look to my past and say, "Someone with my background could never do that, why even try?" or, "You know you won't succeed anyways, there's no point wasting time trying." Or my favorite, "You are too slow, not smart enough, not strong enough, etc..."

Not long after graduating High School, a minor league baseball team local to me was hosting tryouts. I had a few people call me and tell me to tryout and even received a letter from the team asking me to tryout. I was, fortunately, a good ball player and it was certainly noticed by a few people. That said, on the day of the tryout I decided to sleep and say I wasn't feeling very well, so I did not show up. I felt perfectly fine that day and remember it like it was yesterday. I was so filled with doubt and a fear of failing that I gave up my shot to play pro baseball. Who knows if I would've made the cut or not? Not showing up solidified that I would not make the team. I lost before I even started.

When I look back on my life and review all the times that I actually DID take a chance on something new or work towards a goal of mine, it's rare that I have NOT achieved it. I have opened multiple businesses that proved to be successful. I have multiple degrees from college and certifications in my career field. There are countless achievements that I have worked hard for in my life.

Even in times when I was not successful, I was much further along towards my goals than when I had started, and they always lead to something else amazing in my life. I've tried, recently, to force myself to remember, or write down, all my successes. I can go back and revisit the memory or success and build my confidence to try reaching another goal.

This is especially true in fitness for me now. I force myself to attempt challenging fitness goals that require commitment, endurance, and a strong will power. This has helped me train my mind for everything else I face in life.

~ ~ ~ ~ ~ ~ ~ ~

Rather than losing the battle before it begins by doubting yourself, set a plan and start towards the goal. Your mind is an amazing thing. When you allow it to think negatively, you will struggle to reach your goals and start to believe the worst. If you take moments to remember the greatness you've achieved in the past and focus on positive self-talk, you will be amazed at how much you can achieve. Start small, start easy, but most importantly... just start!

"When you feel insecure or like you don't measure up -remind yourself of how far you've come. And in the moment, you'll realize you've climbed mountains and can overcome anything."
— BRITTANY BURGUNDER

I found myself in deep reflection today and landed on my undying desire to always run on 100mph. It was extremely eye-opening to uncover some of the "why" behind this mentality. I spent my entire childhood desperate for attention and built up the idea that "doing exactly what you are supposed to do" is simply not enough.

I grew up watching drugs and alcohol consume just about every part of my life. I watched my mother barely ever work a day in her life and pay very little attention to even trying to take care of my sisters and me. This built up an enormous amount of anger in me and had me questioning her all the time.

"You can't even just try to get a job so we can have food to eat, seriously?"

"Are you going to get out of bed today or attempt to make sure we actually go to school?"

"How could you forget to pick me up from baseball practice?"

Unfortunately, this all built up the idea, in my head, that a day in which you simply do what you should be doing is absolute shit. I was angry, most days, that (what I thought was common fucking sense) seemed so damn hard and therefore felt that it wasn't good enough to just do the absolute minimum in life.

I've since called this (doing what's expected) the "52mph day".

Along with this sense of doing the minimum is crap, also came the idea that I need to do way more than anyone else if I am ever going to be worthy of anything in life. How could I possibly think differently?

I had to work twice as hard to be noticed at home. Getting up, getting dressed, going to school, taking care of my sisters, cleaning up my mom's vomit from another round of drinking too much, stepping in front of another stepfather looking to beat the shit out of my mother – and then taking a beating for doing so- helping my mom go to bed and staying next to her to make sure she falls asleep on her back or side (to help her avoid choking on her own vomit)... these things were all simply the way I had to live to survive... anything less was simply unacceptable.

I knew nothing other than constantly running at 100mph and felt unworthy of life if I didn't. This trait, unfortunately, has followed me ever since. And, on days that I don't do anything extraordinary, I feel like I wasted the day away and that everyone around me will look down on me. I feel like I am not needed, won't be noticed, and will be left to be alone if I don't run at 100mph every single day of my life. So, for me, it's either 100mph or nothing, the 52mph days (average and following through on all expectations) are not acceptable.

~ ~ ~ ~ ~ ~ ~ ~ ~

Like anything that runs at full capacity for long periods of time, running at 100mph everyday eventually catches up with you and you will break down. This is simply not sustainable and, quite frankly, is not necessary.

Understanding your "why" in life is critical when it comes to daily productivity. When I began to realize my "why" is to help support my family and make a positive impact on others' lives, I began to see what I call 52mph is absolutely delivering on my "why" and I should feel very good about that.

When I focus on being the best father, husband, friend,

and co-worker that I can be, while delivering on everyone's expectation (including my own) for each and every day, I am actually moving much further towards my own personal greatness than if I operate at 100mph for a few days and then completely crash.

I try to look back, every evening, and think about my accomplishments for the day.

- Did I tell my wife and daughter how much they mean to me and that I love them?

- Did I help them with anything they needed throughout the day?

- While working, did I complete all the tasks my clients needed me to complete?

- Did I help others I came in to contact with and did they leave our interaction feeling positive?

If the answer is "yes," I put a mental checkmark next to the day and write a "W" because I won the day. My new goal has been to win more days than I lose and continue moving forward, embracing all the awesomeness that surrounds me in my life.

I realize now how much everything I learned and witnessed as a kid shaped my mindset and my action throughout the rest of my life. There are some things I am happy to have with me, but feeling like I need to be noticed and operate at 100mph every single day simply doesn't fit my life now and is not good for me moving forward. I choose to focus more on my daily winning percentage over a longer period of time. While it's my goal to have as high a winning percentage as possibly, I know anything above .500 will keep me on my path to be the best I can be and constantly improving.

"I think everyone's looking for something they already have." – JIM CARREY

No truer words have ever been spoken. When I heard this quote, I broke down in tears. I have been chasing something, who knows what, my whole life. I was searching for happiness and joy and thought that I would eventually find it through things I could buy, or accomplishments and achievements... only to finally "see" one day that none of that stuff mattered.

I finally "opened" my eyes and realized that the world I live in, the people that I have surrounded myself with, and the person I have grown into is what makes me so happy. I needed to focus on loving myself, learning who I was, and understanding that I am enough. Once I started to realize these things, the "chase" for other things seemed to just fade away.

All I want to do now is spend time with loved ones and make as big of a positive impact on everyone around me as possible. I want to help others find their own true happiness and stop "chasing" what society tells us is the dream.

This world we live in constantly tells us that we need more things and that we are nothing if we don't have a ton of money and cool stuff. There are reminders all around us from TV to social media pointing out the fact that "everyone's life seems better than mine" and therefore we always want more.

Without finding personal fulfillment and loving the person

you are and all that surrounds you, nothing will ever be good enough and the chase will continue, just like society wants it to.

Spend time focusing on yourself and how little you truly need to be happy and you will be amazed how quickly the bullshit we seem to think matters actually matters very little.

~ ~ ~ ~ ~ ~ ~ ~ ~

We live in a massive world and we are only around for a VERY short amount of time. How sad would it be if we spent every year of our life chasing something that proved to be a complete waste of time? Chasing and searching for something that we could never find, because it was a thing that didn't exist.

I believe most people just want to feel happy and fulfilled in life but think it takes more money or more "things" to feel that way. I used to feel that way. I used to think that I needed to have more of everything and then finally, someday, some magical moment later in life, the things I had accumulated would suddenly make me feel happy and fulfilled, like I would wake up on my yacht one day and a light would go off in my head telling me that I can be happy now. What I didn't realize was that chasing more things never really ends and never really brought me any more happiness than when I had less.

I remember talking with my wife a couple years ago, when I was making a lot of money, that I didn't feel any different than when we were making ten times less, barely paying any bills and had a baby on the way. It made no sense to me at all. I wondered why, with all this stuff and money, didn't I feel differently.

I finally know now what I wish I knew then...things do not provide fulfillment, people and experiences do, and you need to start with yourself. Once I started to love myself, I could then start to love everything in my life and the entire world began to open to me. Everything I ever wanted and chased to have was always within me the entire time. I am fortunate to have found it and hope you do too.

"If there is no enemy within, the enemy outside can do no harm." – AFRICAN PROVERB

Everyone tries to train themselves to be the best person they can be through physical fitness or education. We spend years and a ton of money going to school to learn how to read and write, math, science, and a bunch of other academics. We join fitness centers and hire personal trainers and nutritionists to help our bodies get stronger.

We focus all of our attention on the outside world and everything around us. We are constantly preparing ourselves for "battle" with an opposition we expect to come from outside our ourselves, only to realize it's our inner thoughts and mindset that control us and can/will destroy us if not attended to.

Our minds fill us with doubt and insecurities. We walk through life making assumptions of how others look at us causing reactions that typically do not fit the circumstances. We form biases all throughout our lives that formulate our opinions on every situation we come across, even if we have never faced the current situations before in our lives.

I have spent most of my life feeling like a fraud because of my childhood. I spent most of my childhood watching drugs and alcohol ruin my mother and therefore causing pain in my life. My entire childhood was filled with broken promises, crushed dreams, and struggle. I also spent most years fighting to survive, hoping my mother would live through the night, and praying my stepfathers or new boyfriends of my mother wouldn't rape my mother or sisters or beat the crap out of me again. We were poor, sometime homeless, and never knew where our next meal would come from. I wore the same clothes many days in a row, would go days without bathing, and had to explain bumps and bruises all the times. The court system kept placing us in new homes, only to take us out and force us back with my mother and her toxic life, until she went back to jail or rehab and then continue the cycle. I witnessed murders, rape, prostitution, arson, and had many people try to kill me, all before the age of fifteen.

All of this formulated a mindset so dark within my head and had me believing that I must be what I witnessed growing up, someone who will always be poor and taken advantage of, who could not possibly ever be a productive person in society, and that I just need to hurry up and get through life so it ends as fast as possible.

I grew up angry and found myself self-sabotaging absolutely everything. I found it hard to get close to people emotionally, even though I would basically fall for anyone who would show me any care at all, therefore becoming attached to people quickly.

Even with good people coming into my life, opportunities coming my way, or many successful events happening to and because of me, my mind still had me feeling inadequate and worthless for most of my life. My inner enemy dominated.

~ ~ ~ ~ ~ ~ ~ ~

I spent years in counseling and therapy. Most of the time I simply said what I thought they wanted to hear. I'd share tiny pieces of my story and move on telling them that they had been very helpful.

Things changed after my father died in a car accident, only thirty days after he met my now wife and we told him he would soon be a grandfather. My father was a good person and someone I always looked up too, but he wasn't in my life for most of my childhood. The court system always gave my mother custody, and even gave custody to my aunts and uncles before him many times. When I got a little older, and could determine who I wanted to live with, my mother would threaten to kill herself if I chose my dad or if I told anyone she made that threat, so (even then), I chose to live with my mother.

When I was fifteen and my mother went to jail, I asked my father, and he said yes, if I could move in with my friend's family so I could stay at the same high school. I didn't see him much again. He visited me for my graduation from high school and then drove me home from my graduation from basic training for the Army. I only saw him a handful of times after that. It had been over a year since our last conversation when we went to see him on Christmas Eve, a month before the car accident that took his life.

That moment changed the rest of my life. I knew I was about to be a father and now lost mine for good. I could never have the conversations with him asking why things were as they were when I was growing up or why he never tried harder to get me out of the situation, or if he did and failed. I spent the next couple months in a cloud and not knowing who I was anymore. I felt guilty for so many things and for lost time. I was angry that he was gone, and it had me questioning everything.

But then I realized I had an opportunity in front of me to right all of the wrongs I witnessed growing up. I became fiercely focused on being the ABSOLUTE best father I could possibly be for my baby girl who was soon to be born. I will be someone who she can look to when she needs help. I will provide safety and structure for her. I will be a role model if she ever feels the need for one. I will NEVER allow what I went through to happen to her

I knew, to do that, I needed to be honest with myself and with a counselor/professional. I started to tell the whole story and, through professional help, started remembering many painful events I had simply blocked from my mind. I began to see that my past was not who I was and certainly did not define who I could/would be. My battle within had begun and continues to this day.

I've spent many hours in the dark dungeon of my thoughts, working to "re-feel" everything I felt when I went through it as a kid and realize that is not who I am today. My past has given me the strength and courage to face everything I come across today as well as in the future, and simply got me ready.

There is no force on the outside as powerful as the thoughts, feelings, emotions, and mindset I have within. I have trained for this my entire life and understand what it takes to keep moving forward. I owe it to my family, I am driven by my daughter, and I am exactly where I should be in life - a successful, happy, and motivated human being working tirelessly to manufacture every ounce of energy needed to be the change I want to see in the world and give others hope.

ACTION STEPS

1. **Use meditation to help you listen to yourself.** Start slow, maybe five minutes a day. Allow thoughts to come and go as you meditate and begin to learn how to listen to your thoughts.

2. **Make a list of accomplishments and positive feedback you get from others.** Keep that list as a living document that you can review anytime your confidence may be lacking. We tend to focus on the one thing we didn't do well instead of the 100 things we succeeded at; use the list to help you remember how awesome you truly are.

3. **Track your wins and losses.** I set small goals each day and then, at the end of the day, mark my day as a win or a loss. It's considered a win if I accomplished more than 50% of the items on the list. This helps me when I am down because I can look back and see that I have way more wins than losses.

CHAPTER 3

PURPOSE FUELS THE FIRE

Find Your Why

"Be who you needed when you were younger."
— UNKNOWN (MULTIPLE SOURCES)

I desperately needed and consistently searched for a role model when I was young. Sure, there were some people in my life that I could look to for some qualities, such as my father (when I got to see him) for his work ethic, or my grandmother for her caring heart, but what I was seeking more than anything was someone I wanted to be like when I grew up. Someone who possessed most of the qualities, if not all, that I thought people should have. Maybe I was searching for a superhero of some sort but, at the time, a superhero was what I needed to get out of the horror story called my childhood.

I, unfortunately, found myself looking at people who would be one thing one day and a totally different person the next. My mother would say "I love you and would do anything to make you happy" only to follow it up the next day with leaving with a new guy to go find or sell drugs and not come home for a week or so.

I'd have yet another new stepfather (my mother remarried multiple times, unfortunately) who would say he is going to help provide stability and safety for our family one day, only to beat the shit out of me for making my bed wrong and beat my mother in front of us to "send us a message" that he is the boss of the house.

I wanted to learn how to be loyal, trustworthy, caring, and respected (not feared). I wanted to understand what it takes to be successful so I could start working toward that in my life. I wanted to get yelled at for doing something wrong so I could learn the difference between right and wrong. And, most importantly, I wanted to learn how to love myself.

~ ~ ~ ~ ~ ~ ~ ~ ~

Many years later, as I sat down to write out my "why", I found myself typing that I wanted to be a role model for my daughter. I listed everything I thought it would take to be a great role model and how important it was for me to live that way every single day for the rest of my life.

I began to realize that I HAD, in fact, learned what it takes to be a great role model while I was growing up. I just had to figure it out on my own and the best teachers were all around me. I learned exactly who I DID NOT want to be and the opposite of what a good role model is.

Here is what I wrote down as my "why":

I want to be a role model for my daughter. I never had one growing up and found little pieces from many people, often times not knowing what or who to trust (rarely trusting anyone). I want my daughter to be able to look to me, if she chooses, as a role model without having to go searching for one.

Because of that, I need to be:

- Physically strong, so that I can protect her

- Mentally strong, so that she sees what self-love and grit to overcome challenges is

- Physically fit, so that I can get to her no matter where she is if she ever needs help

- Have a strong work ethic, so she can see how hard work pays off and impacts every aspect of life

- Trustworthy, so she knows the importance of doing what you say you will do

- Caring and giving, so she understands that true happiness comes from providing value to others

- Loving/Supportive/Respectful husband, so that she knows how she should be treated

- Openminded, so she sees the beauty in seeking to understand

- "White belt" mentality, so she sees the value in always wanting to learn, and ability to seek help

- Humble, so she knows the difference between confidence and cockiness

- Empathetic, so she sees the importance of truly connecting with others

- Passionate and willing to show emotions, so she understands its ok to show vulnerability

- Persistent and "hungry" to be great, so she understands her drive and desire determine her achievements

- Loyal, so she sees the importance of standing up for and protecting those you love

- Brave, courageous, and adventurous so she sees the importance of trying new things and learning what you love and find fulfillment doing

There have been many times that I encountered a difficult situation and had to decide on what to do. I've had job offers that would require our family to move, "friends" who were living questionable lives that I needed to decide on keeping the friendship or not, and many other times that my character and values would be tested. Every single time, I found myself asking, what do I want my daughter to see and learn from this? How does it impact her life? How can I be sure I am acting the way I wish my parents had acted for me?

I live every single day trying to be the person I desperately needed when I was young and I spend most conversations with my daughter making sure she truly knows how much I care (and then back it up with a relentless pursuit of proving it).

"Never look down on anybody unless you are helping them up." – JESSE JACKSON

I remember my father always telling me to treat the janitor the same way you would treat the owner of the company. That's a lesson that has stuck with me my entire life. What's ironic is, at the time, I believe my dad WAS a janitor and, later in my life (shortly after I graduated High School), I also was a janitor.

At the time, there was nothing more embarrassing than picking up trash or cleaning up a cafeteria in the high school I had graduated from only a couple years prior. This is also where I learned the lesson of how amazing it feels to take your time and put 100% effort in to everything you do because it's an amazing feeling to see something in shambles, only to look beautiful and clean after you put in work to clean or repair it.

In fact, one of my favorite things to do now is to mop the floor of the gym that my wife and I OWN. She laughs at me because I simply will not give up that job. It reminds me of how far I have come, it helps center me when my thoughts are scrambled, and it humbles me to remember to stay open minded, grateful, and to take pride in the work I (and everyone I meet) do every day.

I know that wasn't the reason my father would say that to me, and it's certainly not why it's so important to me today. To me, that message simply means that every single person you cross paths with in life is to be treated the same way you wish to be treated.

You never know what someone else is going through, the struggles they have faced or overcome, or what they're trying to accomplish. Also, you never know when you will be that person in need of help and who might come to your rescue.

I have tried hard, over the years, to be open-minded in every situation and work to never assume anything. Sure, that can be very difficult at times, but the more I focus on doing the right thing — the easier that seems to be.

I have also found that I find more fulfillment and enjoyment in my own life when I am giving and helping others. The world seems to open much more and provide much more when I am willing to put others first.

~ ~ ~ ~ ~ ~ ~ ~ ~

While many people use the word "karma" and act as though things always come back around, I believe most use it with a negative connotation. When someone has been "wronged" by someone else, they will say something like, "Don't you worry, he/she will get what's coming to them."

While that may be true, I tend to lean on the positive side of karma and doing the right thing. I truly believe that the people who give the most, those who are willing to put others first and provide for others along their own journey, are the ones who feel the "help" provided back to them tenfold.

I believe we all work in "energy fields" and can either add to, or take away from, the positive energy. Those of us surrounded by more positivity, will be the ones who later receive more positivity. Those of us who provide and surround ourselves with negativity, always looking down on others or believing in our own success over helping everyone succeed with us, will find themselves receiving much more resistance and negativity in the future.

Never take a moment for granted, never assume what others are going through, and never forget that the person you look down upon could one day be the only person who could save you.

"We need the courage to take care of each other when our leaders don't. And, in doing so, we become the leaders we wish we had."
— SIMON SINEK

I'm currently reading "Leaders Eat Last" by Simon Sinek and came across this quote. I immediately stopped reading and just reflected for quite some time. (which as those who know me well, is ALWAYS a scary thing!)

We are currently facing the Coronavirus pandemic worldwide and desperately seeking leadership right now. So many people pointing fingers at each other, playing the blame game and trying to figure out what the heck to do next.

While there seems to be a ton of confusion and uncertainty going on in the world right now, I also see a ton of people coming together (virtually, of course) to help us all get through challenging times, BEING LEADERS. I see so many groups being formed, and free advice, guidance, and support being offered. So many people, worldwide, are stepping up and doing everything they possibly can to donate to other people (whether it be money, supplies, or time).

~ ~ ~ ~ ~ ~ ~ ~ ~

As challenging as these few weeks have been, and as challenging as they will be in the near future, I am constantly amazed and thankful to live in a world full of great people and during a time that generations will read about in history books.

My hope is that the generations of the future will read about how the entire world pulled together and helped each other prevail. That love, appreciation, gratitude, and the constant showing of empathy, are what our current situation is remembered for.

We have the amazing ability to write our story, of how we are remembered, and we get that gift every single day. This is a gift that should not be taken lightly and should always be embraced, not just during the current pandemic. I am extremely hopeful that our current situation will help us all to change our outlook and our approach to life. We should focus on being the leaders, not just searching for one. Spend every day appreciating every aspect of our lives, focusing on the positive and potential for our future.

"If you can't find a good role model, be one."
— GALE ANNE HURD

I've struggled with this my entire life. I don't believe I have ever truly had someone in my life for a consistent period of time that I would truly call my role model. I always looked up to my dad, mostly because he was my dad, and I can remember him being a very hard worker. We, unfortunately, didn't have a ton of time together as I moved back and forth between him, my mom, aunts, grandparents, and seemingly anyone else who the court felt should have possession of me, when I was young.

Moving that often and tearing apart so many relationships makes it very difficult to build trust and truly get to know people, therefore making it hard to find a real role model.

I have certainly always "chased" the idea of finding one. Which is why I think I have put so much time and effort in to trying to be one for others. I absolutely love helping other people and offering my guidance whenever I can. I also try to do everything in my power to show my daughter what a role model should look like. Sure, I have plenty of flaws and have made many mistakes, but I think I have plenty of good character traits that a role model should have.

I treat people well, work hard, try to avoid excuses, try to be open-minded, I'm loyal, operate with integrity, I'm trustworthy, and many other things I always thought were critical to being a great role model.

That said, this is an ever changing and ongoing endeavor — to be a good role model. It's something that gets me up in the morning and pushes me through difficult times. I have to always be working towards becoming the best version of myself possible through education, mental and physical fitness, and emotional improvement. Being a good role model is the absolute best motivation to be my best self which in turn, has seemingly made ME the best role model for ME.

~ ~ ~ ~ ~ ~ ~ ~ ~

I think having a good role model is important for everyone. The best part about a role model is that you can choose who you want it to be. I think I have always struggled to find one because I have struggled to determine who I want to be and maybe set too high of an expectation on what a role model should be.

I think I spent so much time trying to find someone, one person, who possessed every single possible "best" character trait that I missed out on the fact that I can pick and choose MULTIPLE people. Each may possess one or two of the MANY traits I am looking to learn from.

Spend time thinking of WHO you want to be and what you want in life, then seek out people who have been there and done that and those that you may be able to learn from.

Most importantly, focus on being the best you first and being someone that others may want to learn from. You'd be amazed how much happier and fulfilled you will be when you are focused on making a positive impact in others' lives.

> **"Change will not come if we wait for some other person or some other time. We are the ones we've been waiting for. We are the change that we seek." – BARACK OBAMA**

No matter how far I have come, or how motivated I feel from time to time... I still find myself looking around hoping someone will help push me or (dare I admit it) carry me from time to time. Ironically, when I find myself thinking that way is when I feel myself falling deep into a rut or even feeling depressed.

We seem to live in an era where everyone assumes someone will come out of nowhere and "save us" or do it for us. That mentality slows us all down and feels like it absolutely crushes me.

I get tired, though. I feel exhausted from time to time. It's especially hard going on each ay pretending that everything feels so great inside and that I am super excited to put in hours of work. That's simply not the case. And after putting on the show for hours upon hours, I tend to crash from time to time.

When I feel myself feeling sorry for myself, or wishing others would carry me, is when my mind starts to feel shame. I start to feel like crap for wishing others would come to my rescue. It hurts my confidence and leaves me questioning absolutely everything I do. I find that I struggle sleeping, which makes it hard to get out of bed, and then being productive is nearly impossible.

~ ~ ~ ~ ~ ~ ~ ~

I decided to focus more on the journey and embracing the process when I feel myself wishing for others to save me. When I feel the sense of entitlement or panic coming on, I go back to this quote, specifically the "We are the ones we've been waiting for" portion.

No one owes me anything and no one knows me, or what I need, more than me. I have, and always will have, the strength and ability to pull myself out of anything and to achieve greatness. I have definitely been through worse things in my life than I have faced recently or can imagine facing later in life.

While the mirror can be my greatest enemy from time to time,

I know it's what I see in the mirror that has always been there for me and I can overcome anything.

I will not shut people out of my life, nor will I dismiss help when it's needed, but I will never again depend on or find myself wishing for, someone to come and save me. The fairytales we watched as kids are simply that, fairy tales. It's time to embrace the process, enjoy every moment we get, and kick the crap out of our goals.

> **"People are like dirt. They can either nourish you and help you grow as a person or they can stunt your growth and make you wilt and die." - PLATO**

When I was a sophomore in high school, my guidance counselor pulled me aside to tell me that I desperately needed to learn a trade because I certainly wasn't going to college and most likely would never make anything of myself.

At the time, I remember being shocked and angry. "How could someone who is supposed to be helping and guiding me say something like this to me?" I stopped going to him for any help and decided to just do things on my own. I spent years following that interaction telling other people about the event and how clueless he clearly was. I said that he must've hated his job and just wanted to take it out on me. I decided to not surround myself with people like that anymore and only wanted to be near people that would encourage me.

Recently, though, I've looked at that interaction from a completely different perspective. I started to change my views after complaining about how most people in my life, now, simply tell me I can do anything I try to do and never give me any pushback or constructive criticism. I found myself feeling alone in making major career and life decisions because I wasn't sure I had people in my life who would call me out for some potentially terrible ideas.

I started thinking back to that event in high school and realized that my guidance counselor was actually telling me the way he saw it at that moment. What had I done to give him any other impression? My grades were not bad, but had definitely started to drop, my attitude and anger had me suspended from school many times, and I had quit all sports. I was on the verge of falling pretty far down the negative path. I certainly did not realize it at the time, but he was actually giving me the advice I really needed to hear at that moment.

While the message may be difficult, perspective on the situation is critical when you are determining who you should listen to and who you should ignore.

~ ~ ~ ~ ~ ~ ~ ~ ~

I think this Plato quote has multiple meanings. On one side is the fact that people who are in your life can weigh you down through negative talk or actions or simply by not inspiring you to grow. They can also be helpful, lead by example, give you uplifting messages and push you to accomplish things you never thought were possible.

It also tells me that we, mostly, have a choice. Especially as we enter adulthood and can make more decisions for ourselves. We have the choice as to who we have in our lives and what their messages mean to us. We can choose to be around people who are constantly negative and finding the worst in every situation, creating excuses for what they are missing out on and simply not growing at all. Or, we can choose to surround ourselves with people we look up to, who lead by example, and create an amazing positive atmosphere for us to grow in.

If you don't take time to review your surroundings and pay close attention to the people you are constantly with, you may never truly understand what value they bring into your life. Be sure to only allow people in your life that help you become the best version of yourself and (more importantly), make sure you do the same for them.

**"The humble person flows with the current,
while the ego seeks to swim against it."**
– UNKNOWN

Trying to plan out and control everything, or as much as possible, in my life has always been the way I live. It, unfortunately, has also always caused a great deal of pressure and anxiety in my life. I would get extremely rigid in my day and fail to embrace all the wonderful things around me.

I spent years putting up a wall of "strength" or so I thought. I felt that vulnerability was a weakness and control was the absolute strength I needed. This approach was instilled in me at an early age when I controlled nothing and had life happening to me every moment of every day.

I couldn't control whether my mother would continue to battle with addiction or if my stepfathers would abuse me or anyone in my family. I certainly tried, but often failed. So, when I grew a bit older, I made it a focus to control everything so that I could protect myself.

This helped me get through may things in my life and may had led to some of my successes, but it unfortunately also caused me to lose many great relationships, hurt other people, cloud my mind on what was great in this world, and never truly understand what I loved about life because I simply didn't allow myself to truly experience any of it.

Having to control everything didn't leave me any time to appreciate any accomplishments or truly enjoy time at all. I'd finish a task and ask myself, "ok, what's next on the list." Or even tell myself that "I didn't get enough done today."

Living this way, trying to control everything, makes life hard to live. My mind was filled with negativity, believing that everything had to be a challenge. More importantly, I found myself believing that my actions and my approach to everything was always the right way and felt myself having a hard time trusting anyone else or being open-minded to new ways of doing things. This, of course, is simply no way to live.

Letting go of control and humbling myself to realize that I control VERY LITTLE, yet can still be happy, has been one of the greatest acts in my life. This is still a work in progress and something I focus on daily, but it has improved greatly over the last couple years.

~ ~ ~ ~ ~ ~ ~ ~ ~

Letting go of one's ego can be a scary action to take because you need to allow yourself to be vulnerable. Realizing that the world is much bigger than you may seem like an easy task, yet so many people (myself included) tend to struggle with this. We take the approach that every issue we face or challenge we are presented with is the biggest thing this world is facing and fail to see past that moment. We miss out on embracing the moment and going with what the world is bringing us.

Often times, when we allow ourselves to let go, we find that the issues we face, and embrace, bring us the experiences we have always wanted. Forcing yourself to always be in control only feeds your ego with a false sense of importance and, unfortunately, steals any hope of true enjoyment or fulfillment in life.

Allow yourself to let go and embrace the moments that are presented to you. Be open minded about what could possibly come next.

"The hardest challenge is to be yourself in a world where everyone is trying to make you be somebody else." - E.E. CUMMINGS

We live in a world where everyone's business is everyone's business. Everything is public and promoted and shared all over social media. It's hard to know what's real and what isn't because everyone seems to be trying to be the same. In fact, when you try to be yourself, and especially if it's different than the norm, people treat you poorly or call you insane and weird, practically trying to force you to change.

I grew up trying to survive most days, in a constant "fight or flight" mindset, and therefore never really took time to figure out who I was. I basically just put my head down and went with whatever I needed to so that I could grow out of the crap I grew up in.

I envied people who had nice things or great careers. I was jealous of the people who had plenty of money and seemed to have everything they wanted. I found myself wishing I could have the confidence that others had and, worse off, found myself hating most things about myself.

I was spending all of my time comparing myself to other people instead of just learning more about myself, what I liked or didn't like, what I wanted to do in life, or what made me happy and brought me joy.

I'd look at myself in the mirror and think, "Man, I don't look anything like that guy on the cover of muscle magazine. I must be lazy and out of shape." Or, "Look at all the vacations that family is taking, and different countries they are traveling to. They look so happy! I must be a terrible father because I can't afford to take my family on trips like that."

I started to think I had to be like everyone else to be happy and fit in. That feeling, and trying to live life that way, was exhausting and painful. The depression I had always had with me growing up, became far worse and my anxiety was through the roof. I spent most hours of my day feeling like a fraud who does not fit in and, "as soon as everyone in my life finds out they will be done with me and I will be all alone."

~ ~ ~ ~ ~ ~ ~ ~

After some deep soul searching, reading a ton of self-development books, and seeking professional help, I finally started to realize that I am who I am, that's pretty damn good, and I accepted it. I stopped caring about what other people were doing and I truly spent time learning more about who I was.

What are things that bring me joy? Where does my energy and motivation come from? What am I grateful for? What do I, truly myself, want from life? And, most important of all, what is my "why"?

I've stopped trying to be anyone else and have made answering those questions my priority every day. If something I am considering doing doesn't fit in with the answer to those questions... I don't do it. If someone doesn't like me for who I am, or doesn't agree with my answers to those questions, they do not belong in my life. Not because they are bad people or something is wrong with them, simply because we are not aligned as human beings and it doesn't add to the positive changes I made in my life.

It's a constant work in progress and some of my answers will change over time For example, as I am comfortable with who I am, it also makes me comfortable trying new things and potentially enjoying them. They then add to my happiness and bring me joy. Or, I try and fail, only to learn better ways of doing it in the future or that whatever it was simply doesn't belong in my life.

Stop worrying about what everyone else is doing. Don't let the idea of "keeping up with the Joneses" ruin who you are. Society wants you to fall in line, but most happiness comes from being outside the lines where you can be YOU and continue to grow as a person and feel real joy and happiness.

ACTION STEPS

1. **Work on finding your "why."** Make sure it's truly yours too, not someone's else's definition. What gets you up in the morning? What do you want to be remembered for? What are you passionate about? Take money, current situation, or any other circumstances out of the equation and write out your why.

2. **Help other people.** Whether you donate time, money, advice, or anything, helping other people ALWAYS leads to more gratitude and positive feelings. Find a cause you care about, call them and ask how you can help. It doesn't matter if you give $1, or 1 hour, giving is an infectious positive behavior and has always helped me to find fulfillment.

3. **Make a list of things that make you happy** — not possessions you see that other people have and "wish" you had, but things that truly make you happy. For me, movie night with my family, while drinking hot chocolate and covered in blankets is time that makes me happy. That's on my list, start writing yours.

CHAPTER 4

JUST SHOW UP

Get Started

"The way to get started is to quit talking and begin doing." – WALT DISNEY

I was not set to start the challenge of writing this book until April 1st, but then I realized (after reading this quote that popped on to my Facebook feed) that I should just get started now. The easiest way to NOT accomplish a goal is by never actually starting. I have every intention of kicking the shit out of my goals, so I just got started.

There are a million reasons to wait to get started. Some people spend so much time telling others that they are GOING to do something and then that something never ends up happening.

Honestly, writing a book is something I have been talking about for well over ten years now. I told a bunch of people my idea for the book. I would write down a couple of lines that I "absolutely must have" in the book. Then a day would pass by and no book writing had been started.

I also found myself wanting to have the perfect title before I started writing anything. Or I needed real direction and inspiration to hit me. Only to then feel like a million ideas had hit me at once, become overwhelmed, then turn to pizza and ice cream to help forget about being overwhelmed (yet, still no book writing.)

Sadly, the book is only one of the many things I either put off or never got to. Just like many people, I spent more time thinking about great things than actually ever attempting to do then. There are a million reasons why, but it all comes down to the fact that I never really jumped in and got started.

If you find yourself with a passion to do something or a goal you'd like to hit, just get started. No matter how small the step, or how little you do, it's going to move you in the direction you want to be going.

The world, unfortunately, waits for absolutely no one. I hate to say this but, you are included in the "no one" part of that statement. Get to the gym, buy the food on the diet plan, take out a pen and paper, and just get started, you'll be amazed by the progress you will make by simply shutting your mouth and doing the work.

"Ability is what you're capable of doing. Motivation determines what you do. Attitude determines how well you do it." – LOU HOLTZ

It's amazing how much this is completely taken for granted,

the fact that your attitude determines how far you will go and what achievements you will attain. I've set so many goals for myself over the years that I absolutely had the ability to do, and motivation to achieve, but my mental state – my attitude, held me back.

My attitude completely determines whether I will be successful or not. When I am "all in" and determined to move forward, and have the right approach towards my mindset, I know I can achieve anything I set out to achieve. I have proven to myself time after time during my life. My attitude, towards life, when I was growing up with nothing, was that I absolutely will be successful in life and will be remembered for my perseverance through everything. I have been determined to make a positive impact on everyone around me for my entire life. While I have made millions of mistakes along the way, just like everyone else, my attitude has been what kept me moving forward.

I set a few difficult goals for myself very recently and have found myself with plenty of time to test my attitude. My goals are mostly mindset related and take a full commitment to achieve.

For these goals, my ability will not be tested all that much. Sure, some things will be more difficult than others, but none of these goals require some ability that I simply do not possess.

My motivation, especially in the beginning of my journey towards these goals, is running at a very high level. I'm typically motivated to accomplish something all the time. Motivation will help carry the drive to succeed, but it doesn't get me started.

While ability and motivation are the vehicle and the engine to the car, attitude is the key that gets it all going and continuing to move. When my mindset is positive and energized, nothing can stop me. When I allow my attitude to be that of a complainer, excuse maker, or negative in nature... it's like I am trying to pull myself out of a pool of cement.

I woke up this morning with a massive headache, tired from a long day yesterday, and my first thought was to just go back to sleep and give up on my fitness and mindset goals for the day. It would've been very easy to lay back down. No one else would've known or even cared, but I DID. I literally told myself, out loud, to get the fuck up and stay true to myself. I have so many great things in my life. I GET to work out, I GET to read books, I GET to spend time with loved ones. My attitude completely changed, and I was excited to get out of bed and get moving. I feel so amazingly fortunate to be where I am in my life, with the people that are in my life, doing everything I am doing in my life. There is NO WAY my attitude will not be positive, excited and fuel my desire to continue on my positive journey towards excellence.

~ ~ ~ ~ ~ ~ ~ ~ ~

One of the greatest gifts we are given as human beings is the ability to choose. We get to choose what our attitude will be each moment of every single day we are alive. We may not have the same abilities as someone else. Our motivation will ebb and flow depending on the day. But your attitude can always be whatever you choose it to be.

Take time to determine what you want your attitude to be

every day. Write it down and tell the world. Speak it into existence and it will become who you are. Remember that one of the only things you can control in life and embrace the f*ck out of that choice. Do not let anyone else get in the way of your attitude. Go figure out what you want to accomplish and what kind of attitude you want to have, then get going!

"If you always do what you've always done, you'll always get what you've always got." — HENRY FORD

While I do believe in letting the universe hear your goals and dreams — through speaking them out loud, writing them down, or even praying for them every night — is very important to helping assist you along your journey, I do not believe any of it will come to fruition without actually working towards them. Sure, some people get very lucky and things "just happen," but most people spend many, many years working towards their goals and then finally "get lucky."

Change doesn't simply happen overnight by thinking about it. You need to set goals and then prioritize action items in order to reach the achievements you hope to reach.

When I decided I wanted to open a gym, I had to start thinking like a gym owner. It wasn't simply just going to the gym to work out and then going home and wishing it would happen. I had to change my entire approach. I started reading books about what it takes to open a gym. I began to run reports on potential income ideas and expenses to expect. I wrote out every single piece of equipment I thought I would need to open a gym, then priced it all out on multiple websites.

After analyzing the cost of running a gym, I started to reach out to other gym owners to get their perspective. I started to attend classes at multiple locations and asked for time with the coach to find out what they loved, and what they hated, about coaching classes at the gym. I reached out to personal trainers to get their thoughts on the best programming and ask them for results they've seen in clients. I asked why some clients found results and others did not.

I asked for mentorship from other gym owners, as well as other business owners. I realized that having the perspective of a gym owner is only one side of the equation. I wanted to learn from people far more successful than me and was fortunate to have some of the people I reached out to willing to help me. Had I just assumed that the approach I always had to starting a business or reaching a goal would carry me towards opening a gym, instead of trying a different approach, I would NEVER have reached my goal of opening Bridge Fitness Pepperell with my wife.

My entire mindset, approach, and daily activities HAD to change for me to have a shot at being successful. I am extremely happy that I was willing to change so that I could work towards becoming who I set out to be — a person who strives to make everyone else's lives better by pushing them and giving them clear action items to be the best version of themselves as possible.

~ ~ ~ ~ ~ ~ ~ ~ ~

It's very easy to fall into the trap of being comfortable in your ways. Change is extremely difficult and requires a ton of dedication and hard work. But, if you fail to recognize that the old way of doing things is simply not helping you to improve, you will NEVER reach your goals.

Yes, by doing things differently, you will fail a few times. There will be days when you look like an ass because you simply couldn't figure out how to do whatever it is you are trying to do. Just like learning to ride a bike, there will be days when you "fall down" more than you succeed and will simply want to give up.

I truly believe, though, that every single great accomplishment and break through is just on the other side of defeat. It's a matter of sticking with what's uncomfortable, learning and growing from every single mistake or failure along the way, and then finding the path to success.

Figure out what you truly want to accomplish and then find others who have been successful before you. Learn from them as much as you possibly can. Begin blazing a path in your life that doesn't follow the same old trail you have always traveled. Most importantly, never give up on your journey. You never want to look back and wish you had tried just a little bit longer.

"I'mma show YOU how GREAT I AM!"
— MUHAMMAD ALI

One of the most inspiring men of all time, Muhammad Ali, preached for all to hear that he was the greatest long before anyone believed he was. What mattered most, was that HE believed he was the greatest. That type of mindset will set the stage, every single day, for who you will be or become.

I believe, very strongly, that the universe will work in your favor, it just needs to know what you want to become. By speaking out loud as to who you are, with many "I am" statements, you let the universe, everyone who can hear it, including yourself, know who you are.

Over the years I have found myself falling into the self-deprecation role and always making fun of myself. My insecurities had me believing that if I made fun of myself or put myself down first, no one else could and I wouldn't get embarrassed or feel like crap. What I have learned over the last couple years is that I was the only one saying these things about myself. I constantly tried to prove myself to other people, when the only person I was fighting against was myself.

It's amazing how statements you make to yourself have a way of coming true. When I identified as someone who was a slow reader, it would take me forever to read a book. In fact, up until four years ago, I had only fully read two books in my entire life. In case you are wondering, those two books are To Kill a Mockingbird and Of Mice and Men. I basically skimmed through or failed to finish any other book I ever picked up.

Then, one day, I said to my wife, "I am going to start reading at least one book a month." I told myself that I enjoyed reading and that I would never fail to reach my goal. As of today, I read at least one book every two weeks, and actually finish one a week most months.

It's also taken me years to stop telling myself I am a bad leader. It's always been my goal to be on stage, in front of huge crowds, motivating everyone to become the best version of themselves. Yet, when I get up in front of people, I find myself feeling like a fraud. I walk away feeling like people could "see through me and know that I am a horrible leader." This became very exhausting because I was hired to lead people and I own a gym with my wife, a place people go every day to work on becoming the best version of themselves.

I finally decided to tell myself, and others, that I am a GREAT leader. That people come to me because they are inspired by my story, can feel my positive energy and desire to be great, and walk away extremely motivated to kick the crap out of their goals. I take time to listen to great inspirational speakers and allow myself to "be on stage with them" in my mind. I tell myself that it's me up there and that people need to hear my story. "I was born to lead!!" replays over and over in my head and out loud while I am working out.

My mindset is what drives me and my belief in myself is why I am a great leader. It's why my goals will all be achieved and it's something I will always pay very close attention to.

~ ~ ~ ~ ~ ~ ~ ~ ~

Pay attention to things you say about yourself, especially out loud. How would you react if someone called you what you call yourself? How would you feel about yourself if you were to say those things to the person you care most about? Take a few minutes, think about someone in your life you absolutely love with all your heart. Now, picture yourself calling them all the names you call yourself. How does it feel?

While I love my wife, daughter, friends, and family with all my heart, I cannot love them more than I love myself. I owe it to all of them, and myself, to always be the best version of myself! You do too, damnit!

Write out all things you want to be for the rest of your life — successful business owner, great parent, great spouse, millionaire. Now add the words "I am" in front of every single one of them. Read them out loud to yourself throughout the day. Read them again just as you go to bed and then envision yourself BEING every one of them. Make sure you envision them so well that you can feel it. Then, wake up every morning, go to the mirror and say "I'mma show YOU how GREAT I AM!"

"Never make excuses. Your friends don't need them, and your foes won't believe them."
— JOHN WOODEN

I woke up to a full day of meetings and other work to be done, worried that I simply wouldn't be able to do it all and, honestly, not feeling like doing anything. With everything going on in the world right now, having to close the doors to one of our businesses, coronavirus spreading like crazy, and the economy in disarray, I wanted to throw in the towel and blame it all on outside circumstances.

This, typically, would have thrown me down a spiral of misery, followed by lying in bed, eating horrible food, and napping most of the day. That, for me, always ends in a 10pm flip out session because I accomplished absolutely nothing and took steps backwards toward my goals. This exact pattern has happened countless times in my life and I had to do something different today.

I decided, first, to just get my ass out of bed. That, alone, was a huge step for me. I then proceeded to list out everything that needed to be done and then got to work on the list. I didn't give myself a choice. My wife and daughter would have zero use for me complaining and providing excuses. Even worse, I would have been showing my wife and daughter that excuses are ok, instead of my intentions which are to be a role model and help provide for my family.

~ ~ ~ ~ ~ ~ ~ ~

We have all heard the phrase, "excuses are like assholes, everybody has them." And we all know the negative connotation that comes along with that phrase. Sometimes it simply comes down to shutting up, getting up, and moving on.

You need to decide, for yourself, what type of person you are going to be and then BE THAT PERSON. Take small steps, weave your way through excuses, and get shit done. It doesn't matter what else is going on in the world. The world, and most people in it, DO NOT CARE what you are doing or not doing. Stop letting everything else control the decision you make or the steps you take. Take ownership in yourself, your path, and your actions. Decide to be a person who makes excuses, and that's who you will be. Decide to be someone who takes ownership and absolutely kicks the shit out of goals, and that's who you will be too. So.... who do you want to be?

"Do not act as if you were going to live ten thousand years. Death hangs over you. While you live, while it is in your power, be good."
— MARCUS AURELIUS

This quote has always felt like a double-edged sword to me. On one side is the motivating message to make the most of every single day. None of us have any idea how many days, hours, or even minutes we have left on this earth so there is ZERO reason to take any moment for granted. I try to live my life as if I could be gone tomorrow. It's always been a goal of mine to leave a legacy behind, one that many people spend time talking about the positive impact I made on them and hopefully how I helped them achieve their goals. I treat every interaction like it could be my last. I have said, many times, to people I am close to that I want them walking away from our conversation feeling like they were the only thing that mattered to me while we were interacting and that they too take something positive away from it.

I believe life is about making a lasting positive impact on as many people as possible. My biggest fear has always been that I am not making the most of my time while alive and that I will not be remembered when I eventually pass away. I try my best to build strong, deep, relationships with the people in my life and hopefully help as many people as possible. It's always been my goal that, when I do pass, people voluntarily will tell my loved ones how much of a positive impact I made on their life, leaving a positive and memorable legacy behind.

On the other side is the extreme amount of pressure living every moment like it is your last can be. At least for me, someone who deals with anxiety at an extreme level every single day, trying to be the absolute best I can in every moment truly leaves me feeling like I failed 90% of the time. I almost always look back on every single situation thinking I could have done more. No matter how hard I try, I ALWAYS look back feeling like I didn't try hard enough and like I left more effort on the table. It's an exhausting endeavor at times. There is not a single person alive or dead who could possibly have higher expectations for me than myself.

Recognizing this struggle has been something that has saved my life. I end most interactions literally asking, "was this helpful?" I seek out feedback as often as possible and I look to those who love me to tell me if I am making a positive impact. Fortunately, I have been lucky enough to have many people proactively reach out to tell me how much of an impact I have made in their lives, but this will not always be the case.

I also set mini goals for myself every day and, when I hit all my goals for the day, I allow myself to feel accomplished. This has also played a huge role in my personal development. This gives me something to track and, by only allowing myself to check something off when I truly have accomplished it, my integrity helps me stay in line with my goals.

~ ~ ~ ~ ~ ~ ~ ~

While the pressure to live up to expectations may feel insurmountable at times, ask yourself whose expectations you are trying to live up to and if they are realistic. When you find that you are trying to live up to other people's expectations, you have found a clear sign that you are chasing the wrong things.

List out your personal values. Allow your values to drive your goals and share these values with a loved one. By sharing your values with a loved one, you can begin to write out goals that are in line with those values and then truly follow a path of expectations that matter to you.

Yes, we should all live each moment as if we may not have many more. More importantly, we should be present in the moments we do have, with the people we truly care about, and with our values taking the lead on our journey. Write them out, list out the people that matter, and capture as many great things along the journey that you possible can. Begin writing your own story through memories others will be excited to talk about when you are gone.

"I'm a great believer in luck, and I find the harder I work the more I have of it." - THOMAS JEFFERSON

A few of my friends have called me out for saying that I feel very lucky whenever I reach another goal or achievement. I'm quick to note how fortunate I am and forget the fact that I have worked my ass off to be where I am in life. No one handed me anything.

I do believe the universe works in my favor, so long as I always do the right thing and work very hard. Maybe that's what I mean when I say I am lucky. I, just like everyone else, make my own luck. Through long days of planning and preparing, to reading books and educating myself, and to practicing every step along the way, I have created my own chances and had to prove myself to earn absolutely everything I have.

I have certainly found myself looking at some people who are more successful than I am, who I felt didn't work as hard as I did and feel jealous. I've even said that they were certainly lucky to get to where they are. That's before I realized that I do not know their situation. I have no idea how hard they worked or what they had to sacrifice. Honestly, I was just jealous and feeling bad for myself. That's the most selfish thing I could be doing. Rather than focusing on the achievement and having it drive me to get there, I wasted time hanging out with Mr. Jealousy.

Now, my point of view anytime someone reaches a new goal, gets a promotion, or is recognized for an achievement, is that they deserve it and I wish them the best. I allow myself to recognize the jealousy I may feel for a moment but realize that it's MY jealousy and not that the other person is lucky.

It then allows me to begin accepting all my achievements as things I earned through hard work, dedication, and through luck. I appreciate it more and it helps build my confidence, rather than having me feel like a fraud.

Imposter syndrome is only heightened when you do not feel as though you deserve what you have. Feeling like luck granted me everything throughout my life has held me captive for many, many years. Thankfully, I recognize my achievements have come from hard work and I deserve every single one of them.

~ ~ ~ ~ ~ ~ ~ ~ ~

You make your own "luck." Never forget that. More importantly, don't let anyone else try to tell you anything different. When you find yourself in a successful situation, take time to reflect on the countless hours you put in to working towards that achievement. Give yourself credit for the hard work.

More importantly, never sit back and hope that luck will just drop off everything you ever wanted. Yes, having a vision of what success looks like and writing out your goals will help you on your way to success, but YOU must put in the work. You must take action and build your path towards success. No one owes you anything. It's up to you to go out there, day in and day out, and earn absolutely everything you want in your life.

Set a plan to reach your goals. Write out action steps you need to get there. Then, commit to doing it every single day. That way, years from now, when you reach the top, you can look back at all the hard work that made you "lucky enough to be an overnight success story."

**"Strength doesn't come from what you can do.
It comes from overcoming the things you once
thought you couldn't." - RIKKI ROGERS**

I've never really struggled with believing I could be successful or that I can accomplish most things. What I have always doubted the most is believing that I can ever be happy, confident, or content in my life. I've always just assumed that I will never be happy, will struggle with anxiety, and will find myself depressed more often than not. The mental battle within my mind, every day, always consumed my ability to believe I could overcome these issues and forced me to be exhausted ninety-nine percent of the time.

Most of my life, achievement came from my ability to try and prove people wrong, push through physical or "work-life" challenges, and just work harder than everyone else. What people could never see, though, was the internal battle I fought and the voices inside my head telling me I suck, I will fail, and I simply can't be happy. I'd push hard in the gym and see my strength increase, hitting numbers on certain lifts that many people only wish they could hit. I'd open new businesses or get promoted at work quicker than most people, simply because I worked harder than everyone around me and found myself in roles that most people only wish they could be in.

Unfortunately, I hadn't spent much time reviewing my mindset and going to the "mental gym" enough to improve in the most important area of my life, my mindset, confidence, and happiness.

I read a bunch of self-help books, spent years in counseling, and had months of time away from work because I was just crumbling mentally. I used that time to "try" and work on me, when in reality I basically just built up a bigger image of myself for the outside world to see...never really working on my inner foundation.

Talking things through while in counseling was extremely helpful for me to let out much of the anger and resentment, I had been carrying with me. Without spending time in counseling, I would never have had enough mental capacity to finally begin working on my confidence and happiness. Letting go of anger and forgiving many people from my past, along with myself, is what allowed me to finally start working out in my "mental gym," build my internal foundation, and completely renovate myself mentally.

I stopped worrying about what others are doing with their lives or how they may look at me, knowing that most people don't care and simply do not waste time worrying about what I'm doing anyways. I stopped worrying about "looking stupid" when trying new things and simply enjoy learning something new. I started focusing on what makes me happy, those around me that I absolutely love and that absolutely love me, along with constantly challenging myself to learn more and more about myself. I have thought long and hard about what my "why" is and what inspires the crap out of me, then turn my attention to doing more of those things (which, in turn, fill me with new energy every single day.) And, I track all of it in a journal, on my phone, on social media, and anywhere I can go back and review whenever I am having an off day.

All of this has helped me to overcome any self-doubt and any insecurities I have about the future. I find myself excited for new challenges and loving the opportunity to overcome even more. While every day may bring a new challenge to me, and a new opportunity to question myself, the foundation I have built mentally gives me the stability I need to build a beautiful "mental mansion" that I enjoy living in and never thought I could have.

~ ~ ~ ~ ~ ~ ~ ~

The world we live in now gives us the constant impression that everyone else is living their dreams and that getting there would be nearly impossible to do. Or, it also provides a million pieces of negative thoughts to push us further and further into depression or providing the supplies we need to justify our self-doubt.

We are forced into believing that happiness only comes from having more cool stuff, bigger houses, expensive cars, and all kinds of other useless shit. Which makes us all believe that we need to make millions of dollars just to buy that crap that, in reality, we don't need and, once we HAVE that crap…we aren't happy anyways!

We have people telling us that our dreams are bullshit and, "that seems really hard, shouldn't you think of something more realistic?" Never mind the fact that our own fears, doubts, and insecurities tell us that NON-STOP.

Allow yourself to shut off the outside world, determine what really matters to you and what will motivate you to work towards being the best version of yourself. Write down all of your hopes and dreams. Get as descriptive as you possibly can. So descriptive that when you close your eyes, you can actually imagine exactly how it will feel to be the best version of yourself. Pay no attention to what may seem impossible. Don't allow yourself to build in excuses like, "No one from my family has ever been able to do that," or, "I don't have enough money to even think about starting something like that." Fuck that!

Spend time in your own mental gym, working on building up your mental strength and begin to force yourself to believe IN YOURSELF. If you have to, remove social media, negative people, and anything that gets in your way. You may lose friends over this. You may lose a job or family may think you are crazy. If that's the case, and people no longer want to be in your life because you believe in yourself, you are positive all the time, and you have hopes and dreams that you are working for, then they simply DO NOT DESERVE TO BE IN YOUR LIFE ANYWAYS.

Get in the gym, overcome your own thoughts of self-doubt, and kick the shit out of your goals!

"With the new day comes new strength and new thoughts." — ELEANOR ROOSEVELT

It's easy for me to find myself falling downward into depression and feeling like the world is falling apart all around me, even when things are great. I get overwhelmed and anxious thinking about all the things that could possibly go wrong. When I get this way, I tend to dread each day. I go to bed at night worried about what the next day may bring and feeling completely out of control of my thoughts and emotions. This, of course, makes falling asleep nearly impossible, only to cause more anxiety.

I spent most of my childhood wondering where we would live, if I'd have any food to eat, or if my mother would live through the night. I was always waiting for the worst to happen. Mostly because my day to day life was filled with fear. Anytime things were OK, I knew it was only a matter of time, sometimes literally hours, before the chaos would ensue.

We had one Christmas morning that started with us, as a family, sitting around our tree and opening the few gifts we had. I was so happy to have us all together, feeling safe, and opening gifts. I did not care at all what the gifts were. I cared about time together, I wanted and craved more of that. As we opened the gifts, mom threw the wrapping paper in the fireplace. She had a few drinks to start the morning and, unfortunately, lost track of what she was doing.

In a matter of moments, we had a roaring fire on our hands, burning the walls and most of the gifts along with it. We were all so caught up in the moment that we failed to notice the fire until it was big enough to cause damage.

Thankfully, only the gifts and a small part of our walls was ruined. No one was hurt. Well, not on the surface. Mom felt more shame, as she did everyday of her life, that she gave in to her addiction and felt like a bad parent. My sisters and I dealt with the shock of witnessing a fire overcome our Christmas morning. And I felt the lasting effect of watching another positive moment be destroyed in a matter of moments. It all happened so quickly and maybe only lasted ten minutes, but it has stuck with me ever since. And this is only one, very brief example, of events in my childhood that were devasting.

I find that most of my life has been filled with the dread of waiting for something bad to happen hanging over my head. I rarely enjoyed a moment in my life because I was cautious the entire time and hoping to control every second, knowing deep down that I really control very little.

~ ~ ~ ~ ~ ~ ~ ~

Finally, much later in life, I started to realize that going into the day expecting the worst would certainly not help bring the best. I started to embrace the fact that each day IS in fact a new day and a new opportunity. More importantly, I allowed myself to forgive the previous day. I forgive my negative thoughts, negative actions, others negative impact on my life, and allow myself to be fully present in TODAY.

Sure, each day presents its own challenges, but when I approach the day in a positive and open-minded manner my opportunity to live a happy life increases dramatically. Negative feelings and emotions only bring on more negative feelings and emotions. Worse than that, I feel the weight of my negative thoughts and emotions on my shoulders. It gets extremely heavy and continuing to get up and move forward gets to be very exhausting. I want to enjoy life. I want to be happy every day. To do this, I have to embrace each day, each morning, as a fresh start and to be excited about making the most of my day.

What I went through as a child were experiences that I simply had zero control over. I was on the bus for the ride no matter where it was going. I felt as though I had no choice and that, unfortunately, stuck with me well into my adult life. It still creeps up from time to time now. Thankfully, when I feel the negative thoughts, anxiety, and worry about what could negatively happen to me now, I realize I'm on the negative bus and I have the ability to get off at the next stop, jump on a different and more positive bus, and continue on with my journey.

Don't let your past rob you of your future. Embrace each and every day you wake up and have the ability to get out of bed. Make the most of the time you have and enjoy the ride!

ACTION STEPS

1. **Force yourself to remember everything is a choice.**
   Whether you get started now or later, is your choice.
   Allowing myself to realize everything is a choice
   has helped me to remove the "stuck" feeling I can
   get from time to time. When I feel stuck, I make
   excuses, I get frustrated, and I rarely move forward.
   Stop for a moment, write out the situation you are
   in, and remind yourself that your next move is truly
   your choice.

2. **Read motivational books or listen to motivational
   podcasts and write out what you are learning.**
   Listen to the same thing every day if you find it
   helpful. Put in the work to build a positive and
   energized mindset.

3. **Make a gratitude list at the end of every day, prior
   to falling asleep.** Prior to going to sleep, think about
   the day you are finishing and list out 2-3 things
   that you are grateful for. Doing this consistently
   will force you to pay attention throughout your day,
   searching for things to be grateful for so that you
   have something to write at the end of the day.

CHAPTER 5

RENT'S DUE

Stay Focused When Adversity Strikes

"Everyone has a plan until they get punched in the face." – MIKE TYSON

One of my favorite quotes of all time. This speaks to our ability to overcome adversity and quickly change course, when needed.

We have all faced it at some point in our lives. Times when things seem to be moving along just as we had hoped and planned for and then, suddenly, something terrible happens and throws it all to shit.

A big outdoor event is planned for months, only to have a hurricane hit on the day of the event. A beautiful family vacation is planned and then you get laid off from work. Business is thriving and then suddenly a fucking pandemic hits and puts everything in jeopardy.

Life has a funny way of testing you and "helping" you determine if you had the right plan and goals in the first place. It gives you many opportunities to prove it to yourself. Will you adapt and overcome, or will you give up? Should the plan and/or goals be changed? What are some creative new ways of accomplishing your goals? What's the "silver lining" in the adversity?

~ ~ ~ ~ ~ ~ ~ ~

I've been "punched in the face" many times, (literally and figuratively). I've had things fall apart all around me, sometimes due to circumstances that I couldn't control and sometimes do to my own dumb ass actions.

Every time I have gone through adversity, I have found a way to pick myself up and continue moving forward. At the moment of getting punched in the face, I find myself staggering and hurt. I am not immune to the pain at all. That said, I use the "punch" to fuel my desire to push forward, especially when it seems like all hope is lost. It's a challenge I give myself every time, to prove to myself that I CAN move forward.

Fighting through adversity is something that needs to be worked on and constantly trained. The more you do it, the easier it gets. Unfortunately, the only way to push through and develop that "overcome anything muscle" is to face REAL adversity. You will only find out what you are made of when you face difficult times. So, when those times come, look at them like they are gifts to help you learn more about yourself and to build the muscle for future use.

> **"A man's character is not judged after he celebrates a victory, but by what he does when his back is against the wall."** – JOHN CENA

I feel like my back is against the wall most days of my life, but it feels even more real today. I get so scared that I will fail that it clouds my entire thought process and stops me from moving forward sometimes.

The funny thing about being "up against the wall" is that there is nowhere else you can go but forward. Today was another one of those days for me. I felt lost and uninspired when I woke up. I wasn't sure where to start and felt very worried that I would just sit on my ass all day and let the world pass me by. Then a funny thing happened, I realized that if I didn't get working on my business plans, stick to my work out and challenge schedule, and move forward, I would end up falling way behind, questioning everything I have set out to do and risk failing.

So, I got up off the couch and just started doing something. I started with organizing a pile of paper on my desk, then it led to responding to emails, grading papers for an online course I teach at a local college, and the spiral continued from there. I felt my back getting closer to the wall, and I pushed forward like I had no choice because, well damnit I don't! I hear so many people talk about "spiralling downward" in life but no one talks about the ability to actually "spiral UPWARD."

~ ~ ~ ~ ~ ~ ~ ~ ~

When times are most challenging and you find yourself

wondering how the hell you are going to get through it, take a breath and one small step forward towards a goal. It doesn't matter how small the step is, or what progress you make, just do it. I believe momentum plays a massive role in our lives and it's something we all underestimate. While taking a step back sometimes can help you regroup, reassess, and move forward with a better plan, you need to be careful keeping the backwards momentum to a minimum. Too many small steps backwards can lead to a major fall very quickly, just as much as the smallest step forward can jump you forward just as fast.

Momentum breeds more momentum, positive or negative. The beautiful part of life is that you can decide which way to go. Have a brief pity part for yourself if you must, but make it VERY short, shut the fuck up, and move the fuck forward. We are all meant for GREATNESS, some of us just choose to go after it. Now, GO GET IT!

**"If you try and fail, congratulations.
Most people won't even try."** — VANESSA JANE

I've always been someone with a ton of ideas for businesses or competitions, or anything that challenges me and others. Many times, I have taken the leap and made attempts to do something. Most of the time I am willing to give something new a shot and typically go into it with the attitude that I will be successful.

That said, I rarely take on something new that I don't feel like I can achieve or something that feels like it will really put me at risk of losing something. In other words, basically every single thing I have attempted in my life has been very well thought out and calculated. I mostly calculate how much of a loss I will incur if things do not go in my favor.

I feel like this has been a characteristic trait that has helped me get to where I am in life and I can look back at many accomplishments knowing that most people would never have made any attempt at it if they were in my shoes.

That said, I am so afraid of failure that I rarely try something I feel there is more of a chance that would NOT be successful.

I loved baseball as a kid and was always one of the better players on my team. But, when I was asked to be a pitcher, and have the team rely on me to throw strikes… I quickly gave up and made excuses as to why I wasn't able to pitch anymore (my shoulder hurts, I can only throw fastballs, I am better at centerfield or third base.) I was so afraid of looking like a fool that I wasn't willing to give it a real shot or even work at it.

I love lifting weights and attempting crazy workouts that most people would never even think of attempting… as long as no one is watching, and I am not competing with anyone. I have been asked, many times, to join a competition team or pair up with a friend in a local competition only to turn it down because of "insert excuse here." There real reason is that I am so afraid of losing or failing that I simply do not allow myself to work out in front of people (90% of the time) and certainly have NEVER entered a competition. I won't join in on fitness competitions, even though I own a fitness facility and train people to get ready for competitions. I won't attempt Spartan races or any other obstacle course type of a race, even though I absolutely love random obstacles and challenges.

While I look back to accomplishments, feeling great that I made attempts others never have, I am determined to change my focus of "fear of failure" and do more things I love to do, regardless of others and knowing that only my opinion of myself matters. Recognizing the drive within is greater than the potential "failures" has always been what made me great and I intend to utilize this outlook in all aspects of my life moving forward.

~ ~ ~ ~ ~ ~ ~ ~

While confidence may build from successful endeavors throughout life, it's the ability to learn from failures that allow us even greater successes in the future. With each attempt comes something new and experiences only add to the depth of your knowledge.

Do not allow the opinions of others to prohibit you from living your dreams. More importantly, and certainly in my own experiences, do not allow the opinions you have of yourself stop you from attempting that which will bring you joy!

If you have energy pulling or pushing you towards trying something new, allow yourself to at least give it a shot. The last thing you ever want to do is look back, many years from now, and wish you had given it a shot, regretting that you didn't. Thinking of a new business idea? Career change? Move across the country/world?

Start to write out everything you think it would take to give it a go. Then take action, working on it step by step. If something doesn't go well, write down what you learned from it and course correct. If things fail miserably, learn from that too! At some point, during the journey, you will be able to decide whether to continue down that path or not because you will have learned so much. You will, inevitably, have enough information to make an educated decision. If you never try it, you are simply giving up prior to ever beginning and will forever look back asking, "what if?"

"You need to be able to be comfortable in uncertainty." – JAMES MATTIS

Change is extremely hard for most people, me included. Change typically means a lot of unknowns and it's very difficult, if not impossible, to control. Loss of control, or feeling out of control, is something I have struggled with my entire life.

When I was a kid, we seemed to move two to three times every year. We sometimes moved because my mother went into drug rehab or jail, sometimes it was to get away from someone trying to hurt my mother, sisters or me, or sometimes we moved because there simply wasn't anyone else in town for my mom to manipulate and use for drugs, money, housing or whatever else she may have needed at that moment. Whatever the reason, all I knew was that I had to get ready for another new school, new people, new sports teams, and a completely new environment.

I hated moving. At the time, I was a very shy kid. Having to wear the same clothes every day and feeling like every adult in the school system or sporting organizations who knew what was going on at home just felt bad for me, absolutely sucked. And, unfortunately, it was basically every day of my entire childhood.

I tried to learn as much about my surroundings as quickly as possible. I would observe every exit point in every room I was in, read the audience in the room (paying close attention to everyone's eyes to try and determine who may be on drugs or drunk, and who I may be able to go to if shit gets ugly), and learn the systems of whatever school or town I was in. Learning the systems, to me, was getting a quick understanding of who the decision makers were, what they liked and did not like, and figure out how avoid shitty situations as often as possible.

Some of the most important skills I learned were the importance of body language, word choice, and how to blend into a crowd very quickly (or hide, when needed). And I did all of this to try and control as much of my life as I possibly could.

I certainly could not stop us from moving or (unfortunately) stop most men from beating me, my mother, or my sisters (though I tried many times). I could not stop the court systems from continuously making my sisters and I move back in with my mother — even knowing that my father lived a very stable life. Worst of all, in my eyes back then, I could not stop my mother from turning to drugs and alcohol to run away from her feelings.

Because of all of this, I found myself searching to control as much of everything else as possible. I needed to find as much certainty as possible so I could try to feel comfortable.

It's a pretty shitty way for a kid to have to live his life, instead of just trying to enjoy being a fucking kid.

Unfortunately, at the time, I NEVER felt comfortable. I was never able to relax, and I always assumed the worst was to come.

This feeling never left me, and I find myself wanting to control as much as possible in my life now. When I feel like I am not in control and uncertainty surrounds me, I feel an immense amount of anxiety.

That said, it has gotten much better for me in recent years. I have begun to accept that I simply cannot control everything, and it is because I know I now can choose most things.

As a kid, I could not choose anything that was being handed to me and I was literally stuck in the situation. Now, for the most part, I can decide what I want in my life, who I want in my life, and what direction I would like to take with my life.

This has helped me embrace uncertainty of what could be coming and, at times, feel excited for it. I spend my days enjoying every moment I have and doing things the right way. This helps me truly believe that everything coming my way will be neutral at worst and positive at best. I have adopted the phrase, "the universe is conspiring IN MY FAVOR" and I am simply excited to see what comes next.

For the first time in my life, I am beginning to be comfortable in the uncertainty that we all call life.

~ ~ ~ ~ ~ ~ ~ ~

None of us ever really know what could be coming our way,

yet we all spend most of our time trying to control it. The phrase, "control what you can control" is thrown around a ton but not many people really live their lives that way. Spending every day trying to control everything gets in the way of ever embracing and enjoying ANYTHING.

Take time to focus on what you are hoping to accomplish, plan for what may come, and accept that you really have no way of ever knowing it all. Use the uncertainty to learn for the future. Get comfortable not knowing every answer and look forward to hearing or finding out something new.

It's like when your dog sees you as you are getting home from a long day of work, they are just as excited the first time it happens as they are years later.

Live life with that excitement and get comfortable being uncomfortable, that's where growth happens and that's where life is really lived.

"You have to be at your strongest when you're feeling at your weakest." – ANONYMOUS

I woke up this morning with almost zero motivation and honestly struggling to just get out of bed. This, unfortunately, is something I have dealt with for my entire life. It doesn't just go away once you reach certain goals in life. It's not like I woke up one morning and was like, "Wow, depression, anxiety, and PTSD are things of my past and I'm never going to have to deal with them again!"

Sure, I have a ton of days that I feel extremely motivated and everything just seems to come easy. My energy levels are high, ideas are flowing, and I am extremely productive on those days. Lately, and thankfully, that actually is MOST days, but not ALL days. Even taking time to write this seemed to take every ounce of energy I could muster.

Thankfully, I am able to push myself to keep moving. I have always called this effort "manufactured energy." I literally have to make it happen, otherwise I will simply stay in bed, close the shades, and fall deeper into depression.

It took me YEARS to realize this, the fact that my depression actually gets worse the more I give in to it and the less I do about it. I always wanted to be the guy that would just "suck it up" and "move on from it already." I thought shutting off the entire world, avoiding having to admit I am struggling, and being completely alone would help. What I found, years later, is that is the absolute worst thing I can do.

Now, I think of one thing I would like to do. Sometimes this is something as little as go eat food or watch TV. I know sitting on the couch may seem like I am giving in to the issue, but it makes me get out of bed and travel downstairs to my living room. That movement alone may seem like the smallest of all possible steps, but it's a step towards something positive versus sinking into more negative.

I also talk more about my struggles. I will let my wife know that "the storm is approaching" or "the storm is here." That is my way of letting her know that the unseen bullshit going on in my head is VERY present and I need some help. Otherwise, she may not know why I am nonresponsive when she asks if I am getting up to have coffee with her, or why I seem to be very irritable.

I also tell my daughter. She deserves to know why I may seem off and she also does an amazing job of both giving me space and pushing me to keep moving. Thankfully, she also has an amazing ability to know when a push is needed and I'm ready for it or if it's simply a matter of letting me be for a little while.

While I a highly motivated and passionate about life most days, it has been a long journey to get here and is one that I am ALWAYS working on. I look forward to continuing to grow, push through the depression, anxiety, and PTSD moments to hopefully find that they occur less and less from now on.

~ ~ ~ ~ ~ ~ ~ ~

Ironically, days that I give in and get very little done throughout the day (even though it feels like I am trying to lift a mountain off of my shoulders), I feel even worse the next day BECAUSE I GOT NOTHING DONE. I never realized this impact when I was younger.

This is what caused me to start thinking of "manufactured energy" as a way of life. I HAVE to create my own energy on those days that I am struggling, otherwise I make sure I remember that it WILL GET WORSE.

Seeking professional help is by far the best thing you can do to get beyond some of the mental struggles you face, so please be sure to seek out help.

On top of professional help, find a person or two that you are close to and let them know about your struggles as well as ask if you can turn to them for a push when "the storm is coming." Some other helpful actions for me that you may want to try include journaling, making a gratitude list, working towards a hobby, reading motivational books, and EXERCISING.

When you are in the storm, you feel alone, unmotivated, and helpless but please know that YOU ARE NOT ALONE, people need you, and "this too shall pass."

"Perspective drives performance." – INKY JOHNSON

For many years of my life I had the "me against the world" mentality. I also spent most days with a massive chip on my shoulder thinking I needed to prove myself. While thinking that way may have given me some personal drive, it certainly NEVER helped me to feel happy or fulfilled.

I was so mentally isolated from the world that I never found myself enjoying any accomplishment and never feeling good about anything I had done. This caused me to be very distant in relationships, often times self-sabotaging them just to feel justified that it truly was "me against the world."

I had such a negative perspective on the world that I was sure everything would fall apart anyways. I often asked myself, "What the hell is the point of all of this anyways?" I remember actually saying to my wife, "I hope I don't live very long because it would suck to spend a lot of years just being unhappy all the time."

I was great at finding the worst in every potential situation. I'd win an award and immediately think, "Great, now everyone has expectations that I cannot live up to." Or, that people would only associate with me because they wanted something from me. It couldn't possibly be just because they like who I am or enjoy being around me.

It was a miserable way to live and I found myself in deep depression every couple months. Only to find a new task that I could focus on to help take attention off the negative outlook I had on life. I'd achieve the next "thing" and then history would repeat itself. This happened every year of my life up until a year or so ago when I made "loving myself" a priority and a major focus.

Call it my next task, if you will, but it is one that makes a massive impact on the rest of my life. I have found that I spend more time paying attention to my words and self-talk than I ever have before. I change my negative perspective to a positive as quickly as possible. I spend time, throughout my day, reflecting on how I feel and asking why I feel that way. I ask myself if my thoughts are true or if I am operating out of a negative and "old" mentality that I want to change.

As strange as it may sound, colors have never seemed brighter, days never happier, and conversations never more fulfilling than they are for me now. I am full of energy, excited to wake up every morning and look forward to what the world brings me.

I have changed my perspective on life from things like, "Why me?", "It's me against the world," and "I need to constantly prove myself," to "Why not me?", "Who can I make a positive impact on today?", and "I love who I am, just the way I am."

This perspective has brought me more opportunities than I could ever dream of, more great people in my life than I could ever ask for, and more happiness and fulfillment than I ever thought was possible.

~ ~ ~ ~ ~ ~ ~ ~

Its far easier to complain, make excuses, and feel like the world is out to get you. That said, the drain it takes on your mind and your body can get to be exhausting. I remembered feeling absolutely exhausted at the end of every day, even though I had barely done anything. I failed to see the beauty in the world and found myself wishing it would all go away.

I have always been a big fan of challenges and decided to make positive thinking a new challenge for myself. I made myself think differently. It's something I still work on, every single day. Positive thinking is just as much of a muscle memory workout as bench presses, dead lifts, or back squats. You must commit to the improvement and work on it all the time. Put as much energy into positive thinking as you would anything else in life and you will be amazed how quickly all aspects of your life seem to just "fall in to place."

"Real difficulties can be overcome; it is only the imaginary ones that are unconquerable."
— THEODORE N. VAIL

The challenges we can see and feel, we can plan for or at least try to learn how to overcome them. That said, most of us build up these insurmountable challenges in our minds that are simply impossible to overcome. We tell ourselves things are impossible, mostly because we have not done it yet or they seem really hard. We make our small obstacles feel massive and therefore use them as excuses to not even attempt to beat them.

Our minds are the evil doers in our lives, constantly forcing us to question our abilities and force us to believe that even trying to win is simply a waste of our time. We are so good at beating ourselves that the outside world isn't even needed most of the time. We look at the accomplishments of other people and put together a million reasons why they were able to do it, but we cannot.

Thoughts like: "I'm not as strong as she is" or "She was born into a rich family and I don't have any money" or even "She must have just gotten lucky" help us justify why others have succeeded and we have not.

This mindset is the first thing that needs to improve to ever achieve greatness. And, by greatness, I simply mean whatever version of yourself that you would like to be.

I had always been the guy that thinks of a millions things I want to do and "who I want to be when I grow up" only to write them down and then throw the paper away because I was filled with "head trash," negative thoughts and imaginary obstacles that seemed so overwhelming I wouldn't even try. The fear of failure was paralyzing to me, at times. Then, I began to focus on what is real and what isn't. I'd ask myself, first, "What's the worst that can happen if I fail?" and then ask, "Are these obstacles 'real-life' or am I making them up as excuses because I am afraid?"

Since taking this approach, more and more business and life goal ideas flow to me, daily, and I find myself just digging in and getting started with my planning. I determine what the real obstacles and challenges are and write a plan to overcome them. I do not even give myself time to think of potential imaginary obstacles anymore.

Sure, some of my ideas are not ever going to come to fruition. But, because I at least start working towards them, I am always moving closer to my goals and dreams instead of merely sitting around, "comfortable" which, to me, really means miserable.

~ ~ ~ ~ ~ ~ ~ ~ ~

When you build out your goals, do not stop at things that you think you can easily attain, build goals that are well beyond what you currently feel is possible. Then determine what steps you would need to take to get there. Do not put imaginary roadblocks along your journey, just write out the exact steps that it would take.

If your goal is to be the owner of a multi-million-dollar company, determine what you would need to get there. Research how to start a company and how to build a company. Determine what education you would need and what skills are critical to succeed. Start to act, no matter how small it is, and build momentum towards your goals.

Do not allow yourself to get derailed before you even begin by designing a bunch of imaginary obstacles. "No one in my family has ever succeeded" or "I'm a nobody from a town no one has ever heard of" or "I could never learn enough to be successful" are thoughts that may popped in to your mind that are trying to stop you from attempting your goals.

Your mind is designed to keep you away from risk-tasking, it's designed to try and keep you comfortable. Unfortunately, no greatness comes from sitting around, not taking any risks and staying "comfortable" your entire life. If you want to achieve greatness, you must first believe in your greatness and focus only on the REAL challenges you face, then go kick their ass.

"If your dreams don't scare you, they aren't big enough." – ELLEN JOHNSON SIRLEAF

I have always been the "goal planning" type of person. I enjoy structuring my life and planning out where I'd like to be. Writing out a path to achieve my goals has been something I have always worked on and helped numerous other people work on as well.

Big aspirational goals have always been a double-edged sword for me. At times they have me excited and inspired to push forward with an enormous amount of energy. I find myself driving forward and building momentum along the way. Regardless of success hitting the goal or not, I find myself much further along in my journey.

Then there are times that I find myself looking at these goals I set for myself and feeling tremendously overwhelmed.

Thoughts of, "No way can I get all of this done" or "Someone like me could never do that" creep into my mind. The momentum works in the opposite direction and negative momentum begins to work against me.

~ ~ ~ ~ ~ ~ ~ ~

After years of setting massive goals, starting some but normally giving up on others, I started working on establishing micro-goals that lead me to my ultimate bigger goal. I write out mini steps that build upon one another and keep me moving forward. I try my best to not think about the massive goal after I set the micro goals.

When I first opened my financial planning firm, I had it set in my mind that the business would grow large enough to employ twenty people and help two hundred or more clients within three years. I went as far as listing out every department the company would have (even before having any revenue at all), the entire benefit package employees would be able to choose from, and multiple locations across the country.

About five months into the business, while I was now replacing the income that I had been making while working for a large company, I found myself discouraged that I was not on track to reach the massive plans I had set for myself. This allowed doubt and fear to creep into my mind. I would literally spend all night worrying that I was failing and simply not appreciated (or even acknowledging) that I had already been widely successful.

This fear and doubt crippled me. I felt all the worries of my past and the feelings of inadequacy from my childhood swirling around in my head 24/7. I found myself back in the corporate world soon after.

Thankfully, I realized quickly that I gave up too soon, that the corporate world simply was NOT for me, and that I owed it to myself to give it another shot. This time around, I set micro goals for myself, beginning with revenue needs for my family and minimum number of clients I need to be helping within the first six months of operation.

Micro goals, if planned out well, lead to massive goal and achievement. Start small, celebrate the wins along the way, build momentum, and enjoy the process!

ACTION STEPS

1. **Find an accountability partner, tell them your goals, and create a check in cadence to follow.** Having someone help you stay on track is extremely valuable. I have even set up some "punishments" for not staying on track. Owing your accountability partner dinner or having to do something embarrassing if you don't stay on track may be a couple ideas for you.

2. **Set a weekly or monthly challenge for yourself.** I typically have one workout per week that is extremely difficult for me to complete, something that may take me an hour or longer. I do this to force myself in, and THROUGH adversity but on my owns terms. Then, after completing it, I feel tremendous and have found myself thinking back to accomplishing those challenges when real adversity hits. It helps me to at least have a moment to say to myself, "I have been through worse, I can get through this."

3. **When writing down future goals, break them down in to micro goals and action items that lead to the larger goal.** For example, if you want to lose 10lbs, you may want to start by exercising 3 days a week and following a healthier diet. Write down your long-term goal of losing the weight but add in weekly goals of exercising and tracking your eating habits. Hitting the micro goals will help you reach the long-term goal without getting overwhelmed.

CHAPTER 6

DISCIPLINE = FREEDOM

Maintain Discipline on Your Journey

"A goal without a plan is just a wish."
— ANTOINE DE SAINT-EXUPÉRY

I've always been a big dreamer who has a ton of lofty goals. I remember thinking I'd play professional baseball when I was a kid. I would watch every game, collect a ton of baseball cards, and even play pretend games in my room with a foam nerf ball. I even had full seasons and stats written out in a notebook at one time. While I was busy dreaming and pretending, I was NOT writing out a plan or even thinking about HOW I would make it to the big leagues. Now I know chances are extremely slim that anyone plays professional baseball, but I also know I never really applied myself to fully committing to the goal. It was always just a distraction from the bullshit going on around me.

Unfortunately, the trait of having lofty goals and never really building a plan to get there followed me throughout life. I had goals of getting my law degree, being the GM of an NFL team, owning a (successful) arena football team, and many more.

For each of those goals, I basically just jumped in with no written plan, no true action item list laid out, and nothing more than a "wish" to achieve it. Even worse than that, I never put in any extra time or dedication to achieving any of those goals. I would think about it, write down some fun ideas (not plans), and just hope the universe would make it happen FOR ME.

~ ~ ~ ~ ~ ~ ~ ~

When I look back on my life and all the accomplishments I HAVE MADE, I see a very clear path that helped achieve it. Yes, they all begin with me setting a lofty goal and putting it out into the universe to help me achieve it. But what makes each achievement different is the fact that I was fully committed, had a true written out plan with steps to get me there, and I dedicated myself to doing it.

When I had a dream to open a gym, I started by writing out everything I thought it would take to be able to open a gym. I wrote out everything from the equipment I would need to the type of programs I'd offer. I spent days listing out potential budgets, researching the cost of equipment and current trends in the fitness industry, trying out classes at multiple locations around me, and getting feedback from friends and family on things they'd like to see in a gym and from a personal trainer. I spent years trying new workout plans, new diets/nutrition plans, and different supplements. I then began listing out every single action item it would take to eventually open a gym. The next step was blocking off time in my calendar to work on those action items and continue to plan. From the first day of having a goal to open a gym, to the day that my wife and I opened Bridge Fitness Pepperell, was just over eight years.

Bridge Fitness Pepperell is just one example of many accomplishments I have made in my life. Every single one of them began with a plan to get there. None of them included absolutely everything necessary to achieve the goal, because things always change over time. But every single one of them involved research, time, and complete dedication for me to achieve it.

Passion and wishing will only get you so far. Take time to write out your ideas and then begin to research what steps you will need to take in order to achieve those goals. Dedicate time to writing out the path and you will then determine if it's truly something you want to accomplish. Once you know, and you are ready to give it a shot, you owe it to yourself, and the plan you have spent time writing out, to fully commit to the goal and get going!

> **"Perfection is not attainable, but if we chase perfection, we can catch excellence."**
> **— VINCE LOMBARDI**

I have found myself, many times throughout my life, feeling defeated over the fact that I made a mistake or didn't do everything perfectly. I am amazingly good at finding the flaws in absolutely every aspect of my life, from my physical appearance, to the way I word certain things during a conversation, or even how my desk is not perfectly organized. Chasing perfection has been something I have tried to do my entire life and, unfortunately, spent most of my life dwelling upon never achieving.

For a while I tried to set smaller and far more attainable goals, only to find myself miserable upon achieving them and telling myself, "you were successful only because the goal was far too easy." Rather than embracing the successes, I found ways to minimize the achievements and diminish the work that went into achieving the goal.

I also spent some time setting no goals at all. I felt that the fire within, that had always driven me to push so hard, may have been what was causing me to feel inadequate most of the time. I would just go about my day, week, and month, doing whatever came next with nothing to strive for. This method proved to be one of the worst approaches I could ever take.

Thankfully, over the last couple years, I have finally begun to learn that the process and journey of chasing perfection is really what it's all about. Setting hard to achieve goals is the key to becoming excellent in every aspect. I truly believe this to be the case because the journey towards perfection, the systems you put in place, the discipline to stay on track, and the process of constant improvement, can do nothing more than help you improve. I have found that, while I accept that nothing I do will ever be complete perfection, everything I do will keep me on my path to constant personal improvement and overall excellence.

~ ~ ~ ~ ~ ~ ~ ~ ~

While setting huge goals and chasing excellence are very good things to do in life, take the time to set out a path and create a journey you will enjoy that will also keep you in line with constant improvement.

More importantly, capture the moments and milestones that you surpass along the journey. Write down the books you finished reading that directly educated you in areas you want to improve. Mark down in a notebook when you reach a certain weight for strength training or a desired weight for your body. Keep a bag full of the old baggy clothes that you used to have to wear, but now are way too big for you.

Embrace and accept the fact that you will never be 100% perfect but pay attention to how close you got and how much further along the path to excellence you have traveled. When you face setbacks, after spending some time down the path towards excellence, you'll find that you are still far ahead of where you started. Go set some goals, get a journal ready to capture the greatness you are going to achieve, and allow yourself to enjoy the moments along the way.

"How you do anything is how you do everything."
– UNKNOWN (OFTEN ATTRIBUTED TO ZEN BUDDHISM)

It just comes down to giving 100% effort in everything that you do. From brushing your teeth, to meeting with clients, yard work, working out, and everything in between...give it your all 100% of the time.

This concept is easy to say, but can be difficult to do, for a lot of people. The idea of always giving 100% effort may be a task that is difficult for many to achieve, at least it always has been for me. I find myself questioning if I really did give it 100% effort or could I have done more.

I've decided to take this quote on and embrace it every day from now on. Instead of focusing on that 100% number and wondering, I spend every moment of every day avoiding "half-assing" ANYTHING. I do every day as good as I can and do not cut corners, make excuses, or settle for "good enough."

I would never want someone helping me accomplish a goal and stopping at "good enough" or worse, half-assing their approach and hoping it gets the job done. That's simply someone I wouldn't want to rely on in my foxhole every day. I want someone that values integrity and gives the same level of effort that I give so that I can trust the ALWAYS – not SOMETIMES.

Because I expect that of others, I absolutely expect that of myself in every moment of everyday. I have always wanted to be trusted, counted on, and a rock for those I care about. That is something I do not take lightly and never will. Actions speak louder than words and operating my life in a "always give it my best" frame of mind.

The most important person for me to be 100% reliable to, for me to always show I will fully commit to, and for me to hold the upmost integrity and effort in everything I do, is ME. Always ME. When I can fully commit to being the best I can for myself, every single day of my life, I absolutely know I can be the very best for everyone I care about every single day for the rest of my life.

~ ~ ~ ~ ~ ~ ~ ~ ~

Pay close attention to how you go about every part of your day. Take time throughout your day to ask yourself, "am I giving it my all?" Literally stop and consider that question from time to time. When you are making dinner, are you giving it your all? Spending time with your loved ones, are you present in the moment and giving it your all? Exercising or working at your job, are you giving it your all?

Start to build the habit of recognizing when you are, and when you are not, giving it your all. Pay attention to how you feel in each occurrence. I bet you will feel much better in moments when you gave your best effort versus times that you KNOW you could have tried a little harder.

Also pay attention to those around you. Do you surround yourself with people who "half-ass" most parts of their lives? Or do you mostly associate with people who tend to give it their best effort? You'll start to notice the people you'd be willing to be in a foxhole with and those that you would rather not put that type of trust in. Focus on those you can trust, and you will also grow along with them.

More importantly, would you want to be "stuck" in a foxhole with you? If you don't like the answer to that question, cut the shit and start making some changes.

"Success is nothing more than a few simple disciplines, practiced every day." – JIM ROHN

All too often we set some amazing goals and then jump in

to trying to do 18 different things every single day in order to achieve the goal. What we end up doing is completely overwhelming ourselves, slipping up on one or two of the action items and then quitting.

I have done this a million times. I decide that I will go from one extreme to the other with zero thought to how much it takes to change habits. It has happened with me when it comes to my fitness goals, nutrition goals, education goals, and even career goals. I have been known to "put way too much on my plate" both in life and during dinner.

While I do feel that I am very good at completing many tasks by setting clear objectives and priorities, there comes a time when too much is simply just that, too much!

Lately, I have decided to work on a couple habits at a time. I decided to eat healthy, every day, from now on. That used to mean a very specific set food plan and timing out every single meal throughout my day, including snacks and water intake. Now, I literally follow my "don't eat like an asshole" plan, and eat when I am hungry, spreading it out to basic meals, (breakfast, lunch, and dinner), with a couple snacks. I list out "acceptable foods" for every meal and snack and then just stick to that every day.

When it comes to my fitness, it's just a matter of two separate 45-minute workouts per day. One workout is indoors and the other is outdoors. And then, just like my nutrition plan, I list all the exercises that I can choose from for each work out. I take the guessing out of it by following a plan I know I can stick too.

The benefit of doing this every single day, is that I am forming new habits. I don't overwhelm myself with 18 different things to stick too. It's basically five – six items that I want to improve on. I do not give myself a choice, they simply get it done.

I will introduce new habits after these ones have become things I just do now. And, eventually, I will have made massive improvements in every aspect of my life. The daily repetition helps ingrain it into my everyday life and I absolutely love the process.

~ ~ ~ ~ ~ ~ ~ ~

Deciding to improve your life is a fantastic step. Setting goals for yourself, along with action items to get you there, is just as amazing. It's when you have too many items on the list, and you start to see a massive mountain in front of you, that it can end up hurting more than helping.

Building new habits can be extremely difficult to do and should not be taken lightly. Knowing yourself and how you react to certain things will certainly help but giving yourself an achievable list should be on the top of your mind when setting action items.

I have found the #75Hard challenge to be very helpful for me. It's a matter of completing six tasks, every single day, for 75 days. The action items required for the #75Hard challenge are two 45 minute workouts per day, (one indoors and one outdoors), follow a diet (one that helps you move towards a fitness goal), take a progress picture, drink one gallon of water, read ten pages in a book, and no alcohol or cheat meals.

These areas of improvement may not be in line with your personal goals, but you can make a similar list and get started anytime. Do not add any new items until one of these becomes second nature (a habit) for you. More importantly, don't overthink it, just make a list that aligns with your goals and get to work!

"One of the keys to performance is the relentless approach to daily growth." – UNKNOWN

I spent most of my life creating long term goals and sometimes sprinkling in a few shorter-term goals, then developing some action steps to achieve those goals. I would look far into my future and try to decide on the possessions, feelings, achievements, and characteristics I wanted to have. I would then spend time learning what it would take to achieve all my goals and look for people who had already done it.

What I typically failed to do was look at what those great people did day to day. What were their habits? What were there rituals and non-negotiables? How did they act every single day, while alone and while in public? How did they speak about themselves TO themselves?

I finally started to realize that my accomplishments really come down to what my day to day rituals and habits are. How I approach growing and developing every single day would be the biggest determinant of my future success and my ability to achieve my goals, therefore helping me make the biggest impact on those around me in my life.

I immediately started testing out new processes for myself

daily, based on what I learned other successful people were doing.

What time did the greatest achievers wake up?
What were the first couple things they did every morning?
How did they spend their time throughout the day?

What I started to notice was how much time every single "top performer" spent on improving themselves, mentally, physically, and emotionally, EVERY SINGLE DAY! And, the focus on self-improvement was the most important part of their day, so they made it the number one priority every morning.

They would wake up between 4am and 6am. The first two to three hours of their day involved some sort of physical exercise (lifting weights, running, yoga, etc.), some sort of self-reflection period (writing out what they were grateful for, their thoughts on the upcoming day, who in their life could they make an impact on that day, etc.), and some sort of meditation (deep breathing exercises, quiet time, listening to calming music). They would also dedicate time to reading something that provides further education for themselves (motivational, self-development, or purely education how-to books).

Every top performer I researched made their own self-development and personal growth their focus as soon as they woke up, while the mind was at its best and while the world was quiet. This provided them with the structure to improve and allowed them the ability to (seemingly) get more time than the average person out of every day.

I decided that, if I wanted to be like the top performers I had researched, I needed to do the same thing. I continued to set long- and short-term goals, then backing into specific action items, BUT now I also write out what my daily rituals and habits would look like and have committed to doing it EVERYDAY from now on.

I wake up at 4:30am, have a coffee and protein shake while reviewing all that I am grateful for from the previous day and things I am excited about in my upcoming day, then hit the gym for weightlifting or cardio. After my workout, I finish my protein shake and take a shower. Then, at 6:30am, I eat breakfast, take care of my dogs (spending extra time to roll around on the floor with them), read for at least thirty minutes and then write for another thirty minutes, minimum. At 8am, I review any voicemails or emails I have, responding to ones that require a response, and begin my workday.

This time has provided me with clarity for the rest of the day. I have felt less anxious and filled with more energy ever since I began this daily ritual. While some days are more difficult than others, I give myself time and space to adjust as needed, but never miss my non-negotiables that help me continue to grow as a person so that I can be the best husband, father, friend, and co-worker as possible.

~ ~ ~ ~ ~ ~ ~ ~ ~

Many people spend time focusing on the talents they see their "heroes" or "mentors" have, yet they never spend any time reviewing the relentless rituals and habits those same people follow every day.

You can lift weights to build strength, or read books to acquire intelligence, but you must have daily habits that help you focus on your mindset and continue your overall growth if you ever want to be a top achiever in life.

Most people will get out of bed late in the morning because they feel tired, grab a coffee and then sit on social media or watch TV right up until the point that they need to hurry up and get ready to leave for work. Those same people are the ones who are well known for saying things like "I simply do not have any time."

That excuse is absolute garbage and just a way for you to be your own enabler for mediocrity in life. Start to change your mindset, start to change your habits, build in new positive rituals that focus on daily growth, and go achieve what it is you want to achieve.

"Have the willpower to stay focused on your dreams and dare to expect more out of life."
— GERMANY KENT

This is a constant battle. Most days, I feel very focused on my goals and I feel motivated and energized to get up and accomplish things. Other days, like today, its much more of a struggle and I have to push myself to get moving.

I am one of those people who set my clock ahead so that I really have no idea what time it is, but just know that I am "ahead of schedule." My alarm is set to wake me up sometime before 4:30am, could be 4:10am, could be 4:18am...I have no idea, but I know it's before 4:30am. Today, I did something I haven't done for a long time and something I tell people to never do — I hit the snooze button when my alarm went off.

I heard the alarm go off, felt tired and my body felt very sore. I slept on my left side, so my entire left arm was numb, and my legs had decided they would act as those they were cement, and not body parts, making them very difficult to move. So, my body decided to hit the snooze and go back to sleep.

Not long after hitting snooze and apparently falling back asleep, I woke up (almost in a panic), and felt as though I had to hurry up and get out of bed. It felt very much like when the parents in the movie *Home Alone* wake up and realize they slept in and might miss their flight. I jumped up, shut my alarm off and raced to the bathroom to start my day. When I came out of the bathroom to head downstairs, I glanced over at my wife's clock (her clock is accurate), and noticed that it read 4:28am.

Somewhere, deep in my mind, I had built the desire through habit, that I WANT to get up before 4:30am because I LOVE starting my day early, when most people are asleep so that I can get to work on my goals. I deeply enjoy starting my day with a workout, then quiet time to read, reflect on what I am grateful for, and embrace the beautiful world I am surrounded by.

Something else goes on in my mind when that alarm goes off and I think it's even more important that wanting quiet time to start my day. It's that I made a commitment to myself to get up and work on me. I made a promise to myself a while back that I would make my personal development and health a focus prior to anything else. I believe that, to be the best father, husband, friend, and co-worker possible, I have to be the best version of myself. To be the best version of myself, I need to love myself first, and appreciate who I am, and then I can work on every other aspect of myself (exercise, nutrition, education, etc.)

Integrity and loyalty are two values I cherish the most. Anyone who knows me will tell you that when I promise something to them, I will move mountains (if needed) to make sure I follow through on that promise. What is ironic is I have spent my entire life being loyal to others and always following through on my promises, yet I had forgotten to do the same for myself. When I FINALLY realized this issue, I started to treat myself like I treat others and vow to follow through.

My subconscious clearly knows and understands how important being loyal to myself and holding true to my commitments to myself are. It took over this morning when my body tried to take over and get me to give in. My body was the excuse, but my subconscious and drive to follow through on my personal commit IS MY REASON.

~ ~ ~ ~ ~ ~ ~ ~ ~

Most people do everything they can to not let anyone down. They will find a way to make sure they follow through on commitment to others and "jump through hoops" to be sure people can trust them. Sadly, though, most people fail to do the same for themselves. Ironically, we have all heard the term "treat others the way you want to be treated" and we try to follow through and live life this way. Yet, I believe we also need to treat ourselves the way we treat others and follow through on our commitment to better ourselves, love ourselves, and value ourselves every single day.

Make a commitment to you. Failing to follow through on a commitment to yourself is one of life's biggest tragedies.

> **"Success is defined by choice, and it's the small choices, not the major ones, that make the difference between good and excellent."**
> — MARK DIVINE

It's easy to focus on developing huge goals, short and long term. Most people, myself included, will spend a good amount of time thinking about who they want to be or what they want to have years in the future. Most of us rarely take time to understand that every decision we make, every single day of our lives, determine our future. We overlook the importance of every small decision we make daily.

We basically build our roadmap of life with every decision we make and can look back to see the impact of those choices. I'm not saying that short- and long-term goal planning is not important, in fact I think it's absolutely critical that we all have our goals written out. What I am saying, though, is that we need to pay close attention to every choice we make and make sure that each choice is 100% aligned with our short- and long-term goals.

We should be asking ourselves, "does this decision move me closer or further away from my goal?" every time we make a decision. Doing so will help you stay in tune with who you are and where you want to be in life, call it your inner compass. Too many days, or decisions, in a row that do not align with your goals or with who you are as a person, will have you moving off target and feeling "off." That feeling is simply you telling yourself that something needs to change. It could be a job, a relationship, or anything that isn't aligned with you. And that's when the decision gets a bit more difficult.

~ ~ ~ ~ ~ ~ ~ ~

While it's difficult to understand or even realize in the moment, when we look back at our lives and all the choices we made, we begin to see how much of an impact all of the "tiny" choices we made have actually gotten us to where we are in life now.

Allowing yourself to pause and think about the choice, determining whether it keeps you on track or not, before you decide, will help take some pressure off feeling like you are making the wrong choice. It will also help you stay aligned with who you are and lessen anxiety in your life.

More importantly, is your ability to actually "hear" yourself and learn what it is you really want. Spend time thinking about your purpose. Think about what gifts you have, things you are great at. And follow your intuition, even when others may look at you funny or potentially no longer want to be in your life.

The small choices add up. Embrace them. Appreciate them. And make the most out of every opportunity to make the RIGHT choices.

"You earn your trophies at practice. You just pick them up at competitions." – JOSH LOE

The world I currently live in seems to want to give trophies out to everyone simply for showing up. The idea of hard work and winning seems to be forgotten. On top of this, most people seem to forget that you can't just show up and win without putting in work. Well, most of us can't at least… there are some gifted people out there proving me wrong all the time!

That said, most of us build our abilities through countless hours of repeatable work and practice. We spend time improving ourselves to be ready to put on a show during our competitions or main events. This is true in all phases of life, not just sporting events.

We spend hours learning about our career field and practicing the conversations so that we are ready when we meet with potential clients. We stay up all hours of the night researching new and improved ways of helping people so that we can deliver on our promise when the time comes.

The dedication and commitment we put in when no one is watching is what makes us great and helps us win those trophies when we get our shot, if that shot ever even comes. I have never taken that for granted.

~ ~ ~ ~ ~ ~ ~ ~ ~

The process has always been the most enjoyable part of life for me. I was recently asked what keeps me working and training so hard when I am alone and not actually competing for anything?

I said, it's because I enjoy the process of constant improvement and growth. I'm fortunate to have the physical ability to be able to do it, and I refuse to take it for granted. It's what we do when no one is watching that truly defines who we are.

I hope to never lose that focus. I hope to never lose that passion or drive for constant improvement, regardless of the goal.

I never know when my next opportunity will show up and I want to be SURE I am ready when it does. The only way to be ready is to train for it every single day of my life. If I am not making progress, I am slowly dying.

Get to work!

"A man without a vision is a man without a future. A man without a future will always return to his past." – BISHOP LALACHAN ABRAHAM

Constantly moving towards something is critical to my mindset and outlook on life. I have always found that, when I am not working towards a goal or a vision, I tend to fall back into depression, focus on the past or have major anxiety over the future.

Having goals and a vision of the future help me to develop daily, weekly, and monthly action items and steps to take. By writing out these action steps, I can have a process to follow and it forces me to stay on track. I tend to wake up feeling inspired and excited to attack my goals daily, rather than wondering what the hell is the point of it all and falling deep into depression.

A vision, to me, is a goal of who I want to be in the future. It's about truly picturing where I will live, what I will be doing for a career, who will be in my life, and every single aspect of it. I can close my eyes and see the truck I will be driving, the house and land I own, the charitable causes I will be helping, the people I am spending my time with, and it feels absolutely real.

I combine these goals and visions with "I am" statements, such as "I am a Georgia resident," and "I am a world class motivational coach helping improve lives," along with "I am an amazing father and husband."

Every aspect of goal and vision planning is exciting to me and helps motivate me to work towards these goals. I let my loved ones know about my goals and spend time with my daughter goal planning.

My past is behind me. While I have learned so much by my past experiences, I now understand that those years gave me everything I need to be ready for the future and allow me to embrace and enjoy my present.

~ ~ ~ ~ ~ ~ ~ ~ ~

The world is such a busy, time consuming, and non-forgiving place that it can be very difficult to think past the current asks and needs in your everyday life. The fact that most people can't seem to think past today and fail to create any sort of vision of what their future could be, does not surprise me at all. While I am not surprised by this fact, I am sad to know that it is the reality.

I remember being asked as a kid in school what I wanted to be when I grow up. We were all asked that question at some point during our childhood. Yet, at some point between then and however old you are now, your dreams seem to take a back seat and become a forgotten thought in your mind. Why? What caused it to change?

Instead, we think about all the crap we need to do in the near future just to survive, or we spend our time dwelling on the past. We wake up, hating hearing the alarm clock go off and just wishing we could get through the week without any more stress. The thought of "What the hell is the point of all of this?" creeps into our minds constantly.

These thoughts and feelings take place because we do not have a vision or goal that we are looking forward to. We need to change this and change it immediately. Start writing down your vision for the future. Spend time, every morning, and every night, picturing yourself already living your vision. Think about what it will feel like and make it as real as possible. Start waking up, every morning, thinking to yourself, "I'm so excited to live my best life."

ACTION STEPS

1. **Set some goals and then write out a strategic plan to achieve your goals.** If you need help doing so, find a coach (life coach, health and nutrition, fitness, etc.) to help you write out a true plan. Start small — just 1 or 2 personal goals.

2. **Block off time in your calendar, EVERY DAY, to work on YOU.** Whether its time to read, mediate, go for a walk, or whatever you need to improve yourself, prioritizing YOU is a MUST. Start small, if needed, with 15 minutes a day, but build to at least 1 hour a day as soon as you can.

3. **Write down what your future awesome self looks like.** Make sure it's as descriptive as possible. When you reach your goals, what will you have, how will you feel, what will your perfect day look like, who will be in your life, etc. After writing this all out, read it multiple times per day. Feel free to send it to me and I look forward to celebrating with you when you accomplish it.

ABOUT THE AUTHOR

Ron Lotti is currently the Director of Advisor Success at a financial consultant firm in Massachusetts. He's the loving husband of a fitness and nutrition coach and devoted father of a 16-year-old daughter, but he has also been a grocery store manager, a bouncer, a popcorn popper, a janitor, a mortgage consultant, an RVP for a large financial services company, a coach, a college professor, and an entrepreneur.

The idea for this book was centered around a desire to share his life experiences on paper, a releasing of the demons if you will. But also, to encourage the reader to explore their own past experiences, to reflect on how those experiences have affected them long-term, and to allow the reader to open up about their own demons and begin to heal.

Ron did most of his writing in an extremely busy household with a revolving door of activity including loud workouts, teenage shenanigans, and barking dogs. Ron loves making people laugh, helping out those that are close to him, debating, breakfast, dancing, an eclectic array of music, math, Georgia Bulldogs football, enormous ice cream sundaes, and always being right. He also longs to make an impact on the lives of those around him. It's important for him to leave a legacy, which ultimately led to the creation of this book.